EAST ANGLIA AT WAR

Five lads of the Hitler Youth organisation photographed in London during the summer of 1938. Boys such as these made detailed notes and photographed important installations whilst camping and rambling around East Anglia.

EAST ANGLIA AT WAR

1939 – 1945

by

Derek E. Johnson

Jarrold Colour Publications, Norwich, 1978

Other titles by the same author:
OF DOGS AND DUTY
LEISURE IN ESSEX
WAR MEDALS
COLLECTING MILITARIA
ESSEX CURIOSITIES
COLLECTOR'S GUIDE TO MILITARIA

WAR DEAD AT CANNOCK CHASE

'AND THE MOANING ON THE WIND
SHALL BE THE MOURNING OF THEIR HEARTS –
AND THE RAIN FROM EVERY CLOUD
THEIR TEARS ETERNAL.'

Victor S. Wilson

Text and photographs © 1978
Derek E. Johnson and Jarrold & Sons Ltd
Printed in Great Britain by Jarrold & Sons Ltd, Norwich
SBN 85306 813 5
178 TH

About the author

Derek E. Johnson moved into East Anglia in 1940 as a youth and took a great interest in listing and observing wartime activities. After the war he served in the Royal Corps of Military Police as a War Police Dog Handler in Greece during the Communist uprising and invasion of that country.

He has collected and specialised in militaria for thirty-five years and now runs an antique business together with his wife, 'Chick', in Clacton-on-Sea, under the unique title of *Pennyfarthing Antiques, Coins & Medals*. He has a fifteen-year-old son who is also interested in collecting German militaria.

Research for this book has taken over six years with important information and data being gleaned from all parts of the globe. He writes articles for magazines and also appears on TV from time to time.

CONTENTS Page

INTRODUCTION

The uneasy peace which had followed the Great War of 1914-18 was to last just twenty-one years. With political unrest in Europe and Great Britain only just recovering from the full effects of mass unemployment, a war was, to some, a blessing in disguise.

If the methods of warfare had advanced in Hitler's Germany then those of Britain had most certainly not, for the powers that ruled the armed forces still stubbornly adhered to those traditions and tactics which had seen her through the 1914-18 conflict. True, she possessed a few modern aircraft, ships and submarines but even her great navy had been left to go to seed with cuts in pay and near mutiny aboard a few ships of His Majesty's fleet. All in all things were pretty shaky when Great Britain did finally declare war on Germany on 3 September 1939.

That first year of the Second World War will always be remembered as the year of the 'phoney war' and one that the civilian population took very lightly indeed. As the authorities strove to build up the voluntary defence forces, the average man-in-the-street blithely thought that the whole silly business would be over and done with by Christmas . . . a cry that had rung out loud and clear during both the Boer War and the Great War. How wrong he was proved to be in all three cases!

Unlike other wars that this island has been plunged into, this time the conflict was to be brought to her very own shores. Not since the threatened French invasion of the Napoleonic Wars had the unguarded coastline of Anglia been open to such an obvious danger. True, there had been Zeppelin and Gotha bomber raids as well as a few cases of coastal shelling by ships of the Imperial German Navy during the Great War, but for what was to come during these next six years those incidents would truly be akin to a flash in the proverbial pan.

Derek E. Johnson,
Pennyfarthing Antiques,
Clacton-on-Sea, Essex.

CHAPTER 1

PREPARING FOR WAR

For the people of East Anglia the Second World War finally crawled into being on the morning of 3 September 1939.

'Crawled into being' was in fact the right term, for the world had been watching and waiting for such an event for some months as the Prime Minister, Neville Chamberlain, carried on negotiations with the leader of the Third German Reich, Adolf Hitler. The final outcome proved to be a negative one and at 11.15 a.m. precisely a nation crowded around every available wireless set to listen to that vital broadcast which would plunge Europe and the rest of the world into six long and bitter years of terrible conflict.

As wireless valves whistled and hummed and crystal-set head-phones were jammed into place the nation heard this dry and unemotional statement crackle out over the ether:

'I am speaking to you from the Cabinet Room at No 10 Downing Street. This morning, the British Ambassador in Berlin handed the German Government a final note stating that unless the British Government heard from them by 11 o'clock that they were prepared at once to withdraw their troops from Poland, a state of war would exist between us. I have to tell you now that no such undertaking has been received, and consequently this country is at war with Germany.

'The situation in which no word given by Germany's ruler could be trusted and no people or country could feel itself safe, has become intolerable. Now we have resolved to finish it . . . May God bless you all. May He defend the right for it is evil things that we shall be fighting against – brute force, bad faith, injustice, oppression and persecution; and against them I am certain that right will prevail.'

In East Anglia the war came as no great surprise, for officials and pundits of Whitehall had been trying to arouse public interest in ARP, Red Cross and other defence organisations for almost the past year. East Anglia happened to be right in the front line and if invasion was imminent then this would be where the enemy would strike first.

Those public-spirited stalwarts who always seem to be to the fore in times of national crisis had, during the autumn and winter of 1938, started serious training. Among the many tasks undertaken by these hard-working groups were identifying poison gas, administering first aid, and learning how to organise rescue and medical services as well as herding crowds of frightened people into air-raid shelters and rest centres.

Practical knowledge of the exact types of bombs and missiles one was likely to encounter was by and large rather sketchy and ill-informed for, apart from the rather primitive fire bombs and H.E. missiles dropped by Zeppelin and Gotha raiders during the Great War, the authorities were at a complete loss as to what to expect. ARP units in East Anglia could be seen at weekends training to tackle incendiary bombs, armed with long-handled shovels, a dustbin lid and buckets of sand or earth. In rural parts of Norfolk, Suffolk and Essex a coal shovel mounted on the other end of a pitchfork shaft suitably served a double purpose. With so many buildings sporting a thatch roof, the idea of a fork to drag off burning straw could have only been thought up by a countryman.

Soon, war-talk was in the air everywhere – in fact it was all that anyone now talked about. Newspapers and magazines ran articles on how best to protect yourself in the event of air-raids, make-do-and-mend classes became all the rage and, for the more aggressive or militant soul, all manner of strange ideas and ways to foil the coming invader.

Veterans of the Boer and First World War drew many a free pint during the autumn and winter of '39 as they spun out blood-thirsty,

A summons to war! Just one of thousands of telegrams received by men on the reserve. *Photo: Stan Shelley.*

hair-raising tales of hand-to-hand combat with a savage foe who gave no quarter.

Young children even forsook that age-old game of Cowboys and Indians, throwing themselves whole-heartedly into a more modern form of warfare. That bent twig which had served so well as a Colt '45 revolver or Indian tomahawk now took on a different, more sinister shape. Nazi machine-gun or British .303 Lee-Enfield (depending on your allegiance!) all popped and banged with the help of dried-up and inflamed throats. The most unpopular junior companions took on the role of the now much-hated Adolf Hitler and his Storm-Troopers.

Early in the year, on 23 January to be exact, every household had been issued with a booklet entitled *National Service Handbook* followed by a speech by the Prime Minister – 'A scheme to make us ready for war' – fit men up to the age of fifty could join Rescue and Demolition Parties and Decontamination Squads. Ambulance drivers and attendants could accommodate men between thirty and fifty, and women between eighteen and fifty. Women over eighteen and men over forty-five would be employed as clerks, doorkeepers, switchboard operators, or stenographers in Report Centres. Those under eighteen became part and parcel of a Communications Service acting as messengers either by cycle or motor-cycle or on foot.

By 25 March the first public Air Raid warning sirens were being erected and tested. The doleful moaning sound quickly earned the nick-name 'Moaning Minnie' for the 'Take Cover' signal was emitted as a series of rising then falling notes . . . while the 'All-Clear' was just one long continuous monotonous wail.

Black-out precautions were another wartime chore which had a lot of people worried. As early as July 1939 Public Information Leaflets had been distributed setting out details on how to effectively black-out windows and doors. Sharp lessons learned painfully from the First World War, when Zeppelins and Gotha bombers had flown in over the Essex and Norfolk coastline, using the guiding lights of shop and cottage windows to zero-in on to a target, had been well heeded by the authorities. When one recalls how one particular air-ship commander had 'homed-in' to his Norfolk target using the glowing fire-box of a passing train as a homing-beacon then one can well understand the concern of an anxious authority to avoid similar incidents in World War II.

Black-out material cost 3d per yard and although by today's standards would seem more than reasonable, for many the cost of fitting out all doors and windows of an average size house was to

cause considerable financial hardship. One satisfactory method of
blacking-out doorways was by mounting ex-army blankets onto a
sliding extension built over the whole doorway. This served a double
purpose for not only did it make excellent black-out material but, as
the domestic fuel shortage took effect during the cold winter months,
it also proved an admirable draught-excluder.

In the early days of the war blacking-out consisted of pinning the
material over a window using thumb tacks or large-headed felt nails.
However, when the 'All over by Christmas' brigade realised that this
was not going to be the case, it soon became customary and necessary
to build light wooden frames with material tacked into place. This
way, the frame could be lifted in and out of place at will, for to sit night
after night without the glimmer of a night sky twinkling through a
window pane was more than many country folk could stand. For
those who scorned the more usual sombre curtaining material a series
of heavy wooden folding shutters were built around each window.
These were then painted or stained to match the room's decor or, as in
the case of a Norwich woman, painted with gay floral country scenes
– as she observed: 'I tried to copy John Constable'.

Those who still poo-poo'd the seriousness of the situation and took
little notice of the restrictions soon found themselves in trouble and

Selection of Will's cigarette cards showing the different methods employed in Air
Raid Precautions . . . issued late 1930s.

Left: ARPS Gas Detection demonstration.
Right: Ready for War – 1939 gas masks and steel helmets issued to members of ARP and Civil Defence.

up before the local magistrates. Charges ranged from driving in a restricted area, selling food above specified prices or failing to observe black-out regulations (legally introduced 1 September 1939). Fines ranged from a few shillings to three pounds. This dissident minority soon became known as the 'wish-bone' group for an Essex newspaper dubbed them as 'having wish-bones instead of back-bones!'

With an enforced black-out throughout the nation, night life in both town and country became rather hazardous. Road deaths during the first month of the black-out rose to nearly 1,200, while the number of people sporting black-eyes, and chipped noses, elbows and knees became astronomically high.

Kerb-stones, brick walls and buildings soon sported white-painted corners and edges while running-boards and mudguards on motor vehicles also received a distinctive coat of white enamel.

A couple of months prior to the war's beginning, more Public Information Leaflets had been distributed. These set out instructions on 'Masking Your Windows' and how to wear and care for your gas mask. The first showed how to mask all panes of glass with either sticky-backed strips of brown paper or open-mesh muslin glued into place with a clear adhesive, thus cutting down the hazard of bomb blast glass injuries. The care of the gas mask leaflet stressed the importance of carrying your gas mask at all times. This gas scare was a real bogey to the authorities who had witnessed gas attacks on the Western Front during the Great War. One chap who took the problem to heart decided to set out his advice in verse.

ALL GAS

If you get a choking feeling, and a smell of musty hay,
You can bet your bottom dollar that there's phosgene on the way.
But the smell of bleaching powder will inevitably mean
That the enemy you are meeting is the gas we call chlorine.
When your eyes begin a-twitching, and for tears you cannot see,
It isn't Mother peeling onions, but a dose of C.A.P.
If the smell resembles pear drops, then you'd better not delay,
It's not Father sucking toffee, it's that ruddy K.S.K.
If you catch a pungent odour as you're coming home to tea,
You can safely put your shirt on it, they're using B.B.C.
And lastly, while geraniums look pleasant in a bed,
Beware their smell in War-time, if it's Lewisite you're dead!

John Smith, BSC.

Preparing for this gas war or, as it was officially labelled 'passive defence', left many ugly scars on almost every village and town. One of the major tasks consisted of painting the tops of GPO pillar boxes with a coat of yellow gas detector paint while Gas Identification and Decontamination Squads could be seen practising with enthusiastic gusto on glum and often fed-up volunteers.

On 3 September the B.B.C. closed down its regional services, merging into one programme – the Home Service – which was transmitted from 7 a.m. till just after midnight on 391 metres. The very next day one grade motor fuel was introduced to the general public under the brand name of 'Pool', selling for 1/6 a gallon. Rationing was to be introduced two weeks later. In coastal areas many motorists gave up the idea of motoring altogether, laying-up their cars for the duration. Those motorists who had to use their cars due to business or service commitments sometimes eked out their meagre petrol allowance with a measure of paraffin or the odd moth-ball or two added to the ration. Engines suffered but in those early days of the war one cared very little indeed for such material problems . . . it was enough that one had a motor car to travel around in today let alone the morrow!

Everybody became security-minded, so much so that at bus

stations and garages armed guards were mounted to try and stop the enemy commandeering the vehicles, and private motorists were impressed to immobilize their cars after parking them. Failure to do so could and did result in a heavy fine being imposed. In extreme cases the police were known to immobilize the vehicles themselves either by removing tyre valves or tearing out high tension leads.

Some things the general public just didn't get to hear about, like the stock-piling of food in underground dumps scattered around the countryside (a practice which is still prevalent, for the authorities are always ready for the Third World War), and fold-away pre-fabricated dark brown cardboard coffins which had been ordered in thousands by local authorities. Certain buildings had been designated as mortuaries, many being located amidst council rubbish tips – the authorities being all too aware that with heavy raids on towns, casualties could prove something of a health hazard if corpses had to be stacked near town centres.

Housewives, always the first to be concerned with food problems, set out foraging around grocery stores buying up tins of corned beef, biscuits, condensed milk, margarine and tea. Even bags of broken biscuits – those pennyworth snacks that pre-war kids stuffed themselves with between meals – were snatched up to be hidden away for the hard times to come. Money would be able to buy many of the rich anything they needed but for the average Briton, rationed foodstuffs were all that he or she would savour for the next few years.

The old saying that money can buy anything is very true and in wartime especially so. For those with the necessary bank balance the war could be spent in the peace and quiet of a Sussex or Hampshire village while for those who thought that those spots weren't far enough away from enemy bombers, then the lofty peaks of Wales held some promise of sanctuary as the following Anglian newspaper advertisement stressed:

> Live safely and comfortably during the war period in one of the many delightful out-of-the-way beauty spots of North Wales.

With the advent of war, regulations became a way of life for no longer was an Englishman's home his castle. Under the complex and far-reaching emergency powers his house could be searched without prior warning for all manner of strange reasons, be it the storing of extra food (no more than a week's supply being allowed!) to failing to extinguish lights when ordered to do so. In an emergency he could be forced to leave his home, and failing to take in strangers for food and shelter on the orders of a billeting officer could result in a £50 fine.

Anyone sporting a camera came under close scrutiny of the law, for to be anywhere near bomb damage, military equipment, aircraft (flying or grounded), camps or military personnel with such an obvious piece of 'spy' equipment could land the person concerned in a lot of trouble.

All manner of loose-knit miscellaneous prohibitions seemed to spring up over-night. These banned the operation of 'any siren, hooter, whistle, rattle, bell, horn, gong or similar instrument'. For those who hailed from the great open spaces of East Anglia one of the hardest regulations to endure was that prohibiting the flying of kites[1] and model aircraft. Around the East coast, those amateur weekend yachtsmen who failed to remove their small craft out of backwaters, broads and lakes suffered the hardship of having their boats sent to a watery grave with a series of axe blows beneath the waterline. 'The invading Germans would not ferry their supplies across waterways in those craft!' was the official policy in that respect.

As the country moved onto a war footing the first victims to feel the full effects of a totalitarian state – for this in fact is what Great Britain had become almost over-night with the passing of the Emergency Powers (Defence) Bill – were the poor unfortunate aliens. A great number of these had fled from Europe after the First World War, setting up homes and businesses in a country that they had thought accepted them. Others had joined the exodus westward after the Third Reich was born in 1933. Italians, Germans, Austrians and those of obscure Slavic origins found themselves rounded up and herded into concentration camps scattered around the country.

Here they went before a tribunal set up by the authorities who classified them in turn.

'A' class aliens were interned.
'B' class aliens' movements were restricted.
'C' class aliens were allowed free.

Those unfortunate enough to find themselves with an 'A' classification were housed in the vast Olympia building in London and later in the autumn were moved to Butlin's Holiday Camp at Clacton-on-Sea. Here the camp was run by the inmates themselves with a full-blooded Nazi baron being elected as the camp leader.[2] Later, in 1940, plans were made to shift the vast bulk of these aliens to the Isle of Man before passing them on to the Dominions, but whilst in transit camps scattered around the country many of the inmates suffered considerable hardships. In tents with only a mud or straw flooring, no

[1]The London *Daily Sketch* in 1939 carried a story of spies being captured on the East Coast whilst transmitting coded messages to the enemy by means of a kite carrying an automatic signalling device.

[2]*The Protecting Power.* Eugen Spier.

Rationing had far-reaching effects, not only during the war, but continuing until the early 1950s.

mattresses, poor food, inadequate medical supplies and with no wireless or books, life was almost intolerable. Rationing was brought into being not solely because of shortages but because of unfair trading by a limited number of wholesalers and retailers. Limited they may have been, but troublesome enough to start a precedent, for those with strings to pull could obtain anything at any time while those without the wherewithal certainly went without. With the introduction of the rationing system everyone had a fair share of whatever was obtainable at the time.

In the farming areas of East Anglia – despite stringent regulations governing the movement and distribution of livestock (and dead-stock) – folk never really went without the good things of life. Eggs, chickens, home-made butter and cheese, ham and bacon plus a nice tender piece of lamb come lambing time, all seemed to make the war that little bit more bearable. With the wife making home-made wine from all manner of strange but at the same time agreeable fruits and roots, what else could you ask for?

Not everyone kept the news of such gratuitous delicacies to themselves, so consequently, walls having ears (or so we were led to believe!), mishaps did occur from time to time.

The story takes place in an out-of-the-way Suffolk village pub with a local character known as 'Old Jack' sinking more than enough of the local ale. With his tongue well lubricated he was telling one and all about a very special pig that he'd got tucked away out of sight of the prying Ministry of Agriculture and Fisheries Inspector's eyes. He was planning to celebrate his son's forthcoming wedding in a fine old style. Foolishly he went on and on crowing about how clever he was in pulling the wool over the eyes of the authorities, so much so that he didn't take much notice of the two strangers perched in the corner of the small bar. Not until he arrived home a little worse for drink did he discover that he had been followed by the two men. Approaching Old Jack, one of the pair pulled out an official looking card from his pocket at the same time as saying: 'I'm an inspector from the Ministry and I understand that you have concealed on your farm an unlicensed pig which you have unlawfully slaughtered?' Old Jack was so dumbfounded that he didn't know which way to turn.

The outcome of this encounter is still talked about even today, some thirty-five years later. It seems that the two fly boys – for that is what they were – made Jack load the carcass aboard their vehicle, saying that it was being taken back to their H.Q. as evidence. He was left with the warning that he would receive a summons within the next few days – the last we heard was that poor Old Jack was still waiting . . .

As the U-Boats reaped a plump harvest on the high seas sending many a heavy-laden merchant ship bound for British shores to a watery grave, so too did the civilian population suffer. By November 1941 food rationing was at its most critical with a points system being extended to cover certain canned foods, fish, meat and vegetables. Each eligible consumer was issued with enough points for just four weeks at a time.

If November 1941 had proved critical then by the following January things really became grim with items like sago and tapioca (those two most hated dishes of school dinners), dried fruit and rice being added to the long list. February saw canned tomatoes, fruit and peas; April, condensed milk and cereals; in July, treacle and syrup; August, biscuits, and then in the dark, dank days of December when hot breakfast dishes would have been really appreciated, oatflakes and rolled oats.

With all these shortages and rationing, food became something of a major problem for the harassed housewife. Not only had she to be prepared to cook out in a wash-house or garden shed over a primus stove or even a candle if gas or electric supplies failed due to enemy action, but also trying to make rations stretch out over the full period proved a mammoth task. Newspapers competed with one another, offering columns of advice gleaned from either 'former Savoy chef de cuisine, now doing his bit feeding the boys' or a 'former famous shipping-line chef now feeding hungry munition workers.'

. . . 'If you want to get through the winter safely you need plenty of protective Vitamin A says Dr Carrot' . . . 'Eat more carrots and you'll get it' . . .

. . . 'Health rule for April . . . have potatoes cooked in their jackets as this stops precious Vitamin C being lost.'

Such Ministry of Information advertisements appeared in newspapers week after week and soon children all over the country could be seen and heard parroting the sayings.

Yet another victim of this war was the fine and dainty pure white bread which, sliced into wafer-thin sandwiches, had rescued more than one sagging English tea-party be it in the avenue of Frinton-on-Sea or a British mem-sahib's residency in Bombay. Now, just like the vanished banana, it was a thing of the past. Country areas where housewives had access to the necessary ingredients for baking their own bread certainly fared a little better but 'townies' had to endure a grey cardboard-like substance, or if that became unobtainable resort to the National Wheatmeal Loaf made from flour of 85% extraction. It was described by one Harwich housewife as 'a dirty looking, dark indigestible mass of which only the crust portion could be consumed without suffering violent bouts of indigestion.' She reckoned that if the soggy, almost raw and uncooked centre portion of the loaf had been fed to the ducks they would have either sunk to the bottom of their pond or never flown again, so heavy was the mixture.

With East Anglia's prominent position, and faced with the prospect of imminent invasion, one of the first major tasks facing the authorities was the problem of evacuation. In the first instance it was thought that children, mothers and cripples from the large cities and towns – always a central target for bombing raids – should be evacuated to the smaller towns and villages along the east coast. On 1 September 1939, just two days prior to the declaration of war, such places as Felixstowe, Clacton, Harwich and Dovercourt became flooded almost overnight with the many poorer class families of

London's East End. However, with increased enemy activities during the spring and summer of 1940 in the form of daylight bombing raids and hit-and-run fighters, plus the build-up of the Battle of Britain, it was thought prudent to re-evacuate both 'townies' and natives to safer climes. That June saw railway stations all round the east coast busy with the sound of crying, chattering children as they fought their way aboard gloomy, dusty carriages bound for far distant places.

At Felixstowe some 700 children were ferried off to foster homes at Redditch and Bromsgrove, Worcestershire, while at Clacton and district, evacuees entrained for the wilds of Wales or the picturesque surroundings of Hampshire.

With scenes reminiscent of a Victorian melodrama the waifs and strays were herded together. Shunted from train to train – in many cases without toilet facilities – this unwilling, bewildered mass of tear-stained, soiled and smelly humanity found itself dumped, after many long and uncomfortable and hungry hours, in a town or village which was as strange to them as the end of the earth. Even after thirty-five years some of the tales told by former evacuees make strange telling . . .

One woman who was originally evacuated from a London School to an Anglian County High School recalls that there were so many children billeted in the town that school hours were split into morning and afternoon sessions. Some of the children attended mornings whilst another group would benefit from the afternoon session. Games or music had to be fitted in whenever possible.

After spending eight months at the seaside resort she began making plans for the forthcoming summer.

'Playing hooky from school, long walks over open fields and plenty of fresh air and sunshine was something we all looked forward to. But to our horror one morning we were told, out of the blue, that we were going to be moved to South Wales. This sounded like another country to us. We were very upset. I remember that we all rang up our parents . . . could we go home? We didn't want to move. There were tears and tantrums but it was no good; we were advised to go with the school as it would be better for us. One Sunday morning at around breakfast time we all met at the railway station to be unloaded into the waiting carriages. Once on our way we seemed to travel all round southern England . . . we ended up in Wales about 6 o'clock in the evening, very hot, tired and miserable and wondering where on earth

Above: Evacuees waiting to board the train at Clacton Railway Station, 1939.
Below: A selection of a children's card game, 'Vacuation', introduced in the early part of the war.

we'd come to because as each station passed the views began to get much worse. It seemed as though the lovely countryside had vanished, being replaced by slag heaps and little grimy houses and colliery wheels. We kept saying to each other 'We must be stopping here, surely we're not going any further . . . it's getting awful.'

Eventually we did stop but as there were no names on the railway stations in those days for security reasons, we had to call out and ask where we were. In a funny sing-song voice someone replied: 'Tonnypandy'. To us it sounded like Tony Pandy and we wondered what it meant. We were marched down the street amongst cheering crowds of locals. I remember muttering to myself: 'I wish they'd stop cheering and help carry the luggage!' We really felt that we were at the end of our tether after that long journey. Frightened and lonely I remember passing one house and spotting a tin of Vim sitting in the window. It was like seeing a long lost friend and rather cheered me up. I thought that if they use such things perhaps the people aren't as foreign as all that and it's not going to be too bad after all.'

Billets were, by and large, not too bad but it was really the luck of the draw. Some children found themselves in the homes of the landed gentry and as one woman recalls:

'After the train journey we were whisked away by a bus, which took us far out into the countryside. When finally we did stop it was in the driveway of a large house. We didn't know where we were and didn't really care for no sooner were we indoors than we were put into a bed. Next morning we were awakened by a maid who took us to our own bathroom. Afterwards we joined the owners for a king-size breakfast. The house and grounds were huge and something which I'd never seen before was a central heating system. There were gardeners and farm workers and after school I would help to pick plums . . . I'd never seen fruit growing before! It was a wonderful time and Mr and Mrs G... looked after us as if we were the daughters of the household.'

It was all very much the luck of the draw in both directions. Some nice children got bad foster parents, while some nice foster parents got unlikeable children. At the lower end of the scale we have the two little girls who nearly starved to death:

'From the railway station we were then taken to a hall where we were sorted out by our future foster parents. Smart well-dressed children seemed to go very quickly indeed leaving a fair proportion of the 'other kind' behind. A number of times I was picked out but my friend wouldn't let me out of her sight . . . she had to come also or neither of us would go! Finally this little old lady said she would take the pair of us so off we toddled to her cottage. There we were tired, cold and very frightened and all the old dear had to give us was a plate of cold mutton, mint sauce and dried bread. Very timidly we refused to eat the mutton making the excuse that we didn't eat meat anyway. We made do with the dried bread and mint sauce. From that day on for all the time we were there we never saw a piece of fresh meat again. On Sunday if we were very lucky we had corned beef or tinned pilchards – an absolute luxury. However, this was supposed to be a secret and the old lady warned us that if we told anyone she would turn us into frogs! We actually believed her for after all we were only young. Even when school health inspectors called to find out how we were and why we looked so undernourished not a word passed our lips for we did really think the old dear was a witch with powers to carry out her threat.'

Links with home were slender and obligatory weekly letters found their way home to sadly-missed parents. Many of these letters are still preserved as mementoes of an enforced separation, and talk about food, ration books and the family pets. But not all the children's mail got through as our 'frog-to-be' continues with her tale:

'About once a month my parents used to send me a large food parcel – this being in answer to a frantic cry for food – and the first time I was allowed to open and keep the contents. Not so the others for the 'witch' had seen the kind of goodies I'd received and was ready and waiting for the next one. No sooner was it delivered than on went a sticky label addressed to her daughter in Birmingham. On another occasion after I had pestered my father for a cycle I finally received a scooter. Although it was not the bike I had dreamed of owning, Father had explained that as cycles were not to be had for love nor money the scooter was all he could find. One or two scoots up and down the garden path were all I managed to get before that too was re-wrapped and shipped off to her daughter's children up north.'

Billetors had their fair share of problems as well for among those children evacuated to East Anglia in that first great mad rush of 1 September, many came from large city and town slum areas. Some of these had anti-social habits such as bed-wetting. So concerned were the authorities with the problem that anti-bed-wetting clinics had to be introduced to try to combat the menace.

Parents were supposed to contribute a few shillings towards their child's board but many just could not afford the 2/- requested. Billetors received 10/6d for the first child and 8/6d per head for any others. When it came to billeting mother and child, which was, in fact, just bare lodgings and no food, the billetor received from the authorities 5/- per adult and 3/- per child a week. Mothers had to purchase and cook their own food using the billetor's kitchen. With two women in the same kitchen friction just had to occur from time to time, no matter how good an understanding they may have had. We have cases of complaints such as the estranged mother and baby coming from a good, clean middle-class background finding herself in a primitive outback farming community where the word hygiene had never been heard of, let alone practised. On the other hand, some billetors found themselves landed with a mother who, garbed in vermin-infested rags and with a Wild Woodbine cigarette permanently glued to her lower lip, would allow the grubby child to urinate in the corner of a sitting-room. When brought to task and shown the toilet and bathroom they found both parties using the bath for the same function!

After all these years one can only wonder what all that moving folk back and forth from one side of the country to the other ever achieved. So bewildered, frustrated and upset did estranged families become that many braved the bombing raids to return home. In the words of one of the evacuees who found himself at Stroud:

'The one point that rather gave us food for thought was that we hadn't been there many weeks at this supposedly safe place when a Junkers 88 photographic reconnaissance aircraft was shot down only three or four hundred yards from the school. The pilot, who had baled out, actually came down in the school playground; in the process they in turn had shot down one of our aircraft which had come down in flames and buried itself in the ground some two to three hundred yards away from the school . . . so called safe place!'

And so the human cargo was ferried hither and thither with children being misplaced, lost for a week or more, and even ending up in the wrong part of the country, despite the fact that each child was equipped with a large luggage label which, hung around the neck or pinned to clothing, gave all the relevant details of the bearer. From Dagenham, evacuees went by sea ferried by the old weather beaten-steamers that in far happier times had travelled the same route laden with pleasure-seeking trippers in search of fun and sunshine at the seaside. This time their passengers, bound for Yarmouth, Felixstowe and Lowestoft, were to find many untold hardships including sparse accommodation and food. In some cases teachers and children had to sleep together in sheds and barns stretched out on bales of straw covered with packing or, at the best, grubby horse blankets. Food being scarce, a number of evacuees were fed for two or three days on nothing else but apples, cheese and milk.[1]

During late 1939 the Queen decided to send a personal letter of thanks to those foster-mothers worthy of such praise but it is worth noting that the letter in question was not sent until the following May. Vetting those worthy enough to receive such a royal accolade proved something of a problem for the billeting officers!

'I wish to mark, by this personal message, my appreciation of the service you have rendered to your country in 1939 –

In the early days of the war you opened your doors to strangers who were in need of shelter, and offered to share your home with them.

I know that to this unselfish task you have sacrificed much of your own comfort, and that it could not have been achieved without the loyal co-operation of all in your household.

By your sympathy you have earned the gratitude of those to whom you have shown hospitality and by your readiness to serve you have helped the State in a work of great value.'

Elizabeth R.

For those unfortunate (or fortunate, depending upon your point of view!) enough not to be evacuated due to the importance of their job the authorities introduced a system of trenches and shelters in the event of enemy bombing raids. During the early days of the war open areas in Anglian towns witnessed scenes of frantic mole-like activity as parks, playing fields and even golf courses were given over to trenches. On nearly every street corner one would find a sign bearing just a single word TRENCHES and an arrow. At first it had been planned to make these dug-outs fit for habitation but those who had witnessed the condition of such trench-shelters during the First World War, with trench-fever, lice and other vermin being prevalent, saw to it that other schemes were introduced quickly.

One of these came in the form of the famous Anderson shelter, named after Sir John Anderson, Home Secretary and Minister of Home Security. This was made of two curved wall sections of corrugated steel meeting in a ridge at the top and bolted to thick girders. Sunk approximately three feet into the ground, the top was covered with a thick layer of earth or, in some instances, sandbags. The sunken entrance was in turn protected by a steel shield and earthen blast wall. It was capable of sheltering six people and with clever manipulation with bunk beds could prove quite a comfortable, though at the same time rather cramped, shelter standing up to all

[1]*Evacuation Survey*. Richard Padley & Margaret Cole.

manner of blasts except a direct hit. For those earning less than £250 per year the shelter was provided free of charge while those in the higher wage bracket could purchase an 'Anderson' for around £10 – 2¼ million shelters were distributed free of charge.

One of the major faults with this shelter was flooding, which no amount of pumping or bailing could cure. In winter it was common practice to line the floor space with old doors or lengths of scrap timber – all too readily available in towns that had suffered heavy bomb damage – but after the first initial wave of panic the public in general abandoned their 'Anderson', taking their chances in cellars or beneath staircases. One could hear folk discussing the merits of sheltering beneath the stairs or huddling against a chimney breast. In many Anglian towns which had suffered from the full force of those early Luftwaffe bombing raids, it was very often possible to see whole rows of buildings reduced to a battered pile of bricks and rubble. The one outstanding feature being that in the majority of cases chimney breasts and staircases could be seen standing ragged and proud, virtually unscathed. The durability of those garden shelters was rather remarkable for even now, when wandering through sleepy country towns or villages, one can still see the odd one or two now serving as a garden shed or store.

During the long winter months of 1939-40 Anderson shelter dwellers could be seen every evening trooping into their gardens garbed in pyjamas, overcoats, balaclava helmets and wellington boots, clasping hot water bottles and thermos flasks together with boxes of sandwiches and other foodstuffs.

Children (together with their boxed gas masks) were hustled into the top bunks, drifting off into uneasy slumbers as threatening droplets of condensation gathered in force on the metal ribs above their heads. Paraffin primus and the famous black enamel Valor 525 stove would project dancing fingers of yellow and blue light around the cramped interior while fumes from this primitive form of central heating were allowed to escape periodically by quickly opening and closing the makeshift blanket-clad door.

One reads of dozens of cases where these small but able shelters withstood all manner of blasts and attacks; Chelmsford, Lowestoft, Cambridge, Norwich and many more far too numerous to list individually were very often completely buried by bomb-blasted masonry or falls of earth and sand. Time after time shelters saved the lives of both town and country folk against falling shell and bomb splinters as well as pieces of destroyed aircraft. Unfortunately, occasionally we hear of a shelter suffering a direct hit. Such was the case on 25 August 1942 at Nacton, when a mother and her eight children were killed after their Anderson shelter was struck by a semi-armour-piercing bomb. The father, who had been standing nearby, was seriously injured and three householders of adjoining houses also standing outside their shelters were killed. This latter type of casualty was all too common for a great number of civilians were killed or maimed whilst standing outside their shelters to view enemy aircraft passing overhead or during a dog-fight.

March 1940 saw the construction of brick-built shelters being situated in the larger towns and cities and capable of housing some fifty people. In theory it was a well-thought out plan but, however, with a drastic shortage of cement many were built with a mixture of sand and lime. Not only were they very unsafe; a great number did indeed tumble around the ears of the occupants on the first good bomb blast; but they also proved to be damp and smelly. Not really to be wondered at, as in most instances they doubled as unofficial toilets for drunken soldiers barrackward-bound after a night out on the town. Subsequent improved versions were in fact equipped with a toilet, a damp course and a locked outer-door; the key being held by a warden who lived nearby who would, on hearing the warning siren, rush to open the door and usher people inside.

It was later discovered that many of the earlier shelters had been constructed with inferior second-rate materials despite the fact that the builder concerned had been paid top rates. Prosecutions insti-gated by the authorities produced little compensation and many of the shelters fell into a state of general disrepair. In fact, brick-built shelters didn't really catch on with the general public.

A graphic example of just how unpopular they were can be cited in the following account. During April 1941 the decomposed body of a man had been discovered in an air-raid shelter in Cambridge. Investigations revealed that he was Ter Braak, a German agent who had landed in England in November 1940. Moving into the Cambridge area he had tried to make contact with another Abwehr agent already established on the east coast. Failing to make positive contact and running out of money and necessary food coupons he had crept into the shelter to commit suicide, his body only being discovered the following springtime.

All manner of buildings were utilised as shelters. Schools with stout enough connecting corridors were sand-bagged up and rows of wooden seats installed. Churches opened their crypts and vaults with the living sheltering side by side with the dusty remains of a bygone generation. Museums such as the ancient Colchester Castle – a fine Norman Keep dating back to the late eleventh century built on the remains of a Roman temple – made an excellent air-raid shelter. Many of the valuable and priceless exhibits were housed in the water-tight dungeons with their impregnable fifteen foot thick walls. Norwich Castle also took on much the same role, proving that the old can be assimilated with the new.

And so East Anglia prepared for war. The full truth of the matter was that nobody really knew what to expect. H. G. Wells, in his prophetic *War of the Worlds*, had pricked too readily on the authorities' open nerve, but even they didn't fully realise what kind of dreadful cataclysm would sweep around the world during the next six long and bitter years.

CHAPTER TWO

HALT! WHO GOES THERE?

'I'm guarding the home of the Home Guard'
(popular ditty sung by George Formby.)

Not since the troubled and uneasy times of the Napoleonic Wars, when the coast of East Anglia had resounded to the sharp clatter of the arms and drills of local volunteers, had Britain seen such a buzz of frantic activity. Back in the early 1800s lords, squires and rich land owners had done their bit by raising villagers and workmen into squads and platoons of militia, volunteer forces and Sea Fencibles. Self-appointed officers, garbed in all the splendid trappings and paraphernalia of the period, led their men around the countryside mounted on a high-stepping horse, urging the simple and frightened folk to take up arms to fight off the threatened French invaders. Just like the nineteenth century, 1940 saw bands of men marching and drilling led by well-meaning but very often grossly incompetent officers.

Four days after the invasion of Holland on the evening of 14 August 1940 an important speech was broadcast by Mr Anthony Eden, Secretary of State for War, just after the nine o'clock news. In this he pointed out that Europe had been overrun by German parachutists and to alleviate such a likelihood taking place in Great Britain a new, special force was being built.

'Since the war began, the Government has received countless enquiries from all over the Kingdom from men of all ages who are for one reason or another not at present engaged in military service, and who wish to do something for the defence of their country. Well, now is your opportunity. We want a large number of such men in Great Britain who are British subjects, between the ages of seventeen and sixty-five, to come forward now and offer their services ... The name of the new Force which is now to be raised will be THE LOCAL DEFENCE VOLUNTEERS – This name describes its duties in three words.'

The idea of forming the LDV was not Anthony Eden's but the brain-child of General Sir Walter Kirke and Brigadier W. Garden-Roe. From the very start it proved a huge success, especially around the undefended East Anglian areas. In Essex alone there numbered some 40,000 men by mid 1942.

"Major Walpole here. They've smashed through the road block at Weedon Cross!"

Local Defence Volunteers . . . as *Punch* saw them. *Punch Magazine.*

Unfortunately, enthusiasm as always, tended to get out of hand and we have reports of bands of volunteers wandering around towns and villages armed to the teeth and terrorizing the local inhabitants. No matter if you had lived in a village all your life and even lived next door to the chap in question, if he stopped you going past his check-point and you didn't show your identity papers he would more than likely arrest you on the spot!

In the end worried police authorities had to arrest some LDV members who insisted on marching around the highways and by-ways challenging all and sundry with weapons ranging from rusty old muzzle-loading rifles (c.1854 period) to double-barrelled big game elephant guns. In some distressing incidents the weapons were, in fact, discharged in panic. At Romford, two sentries opened fire at a car which, for some reason or other (it was thought that due to a noisy exhaust the driver failed to hear the challenge!), failed to stop. Four of the passengers were badly wounded and a fifth was killed outright. Because of increased concern regarding private citizens wandering about in armed parties, the Secretary for War, Sir Edward Grigg, explained in Parliament that the prime function of the Home Guard[1] was to guard vulnerable rail and highways, man road blocks and keep watch for landings by enemy paratroopers. Sir Edward also emphasised the point that although members of the Home Guard were in fact under military command they would not, at that early stage, be armed with service rifles but only with shotguns and low calibre sporting rifles.

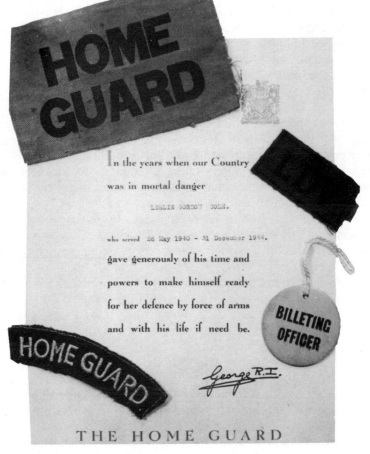

Mementoes of life in the LDV and, as it was later to become, the Home Guard. *Photo: Stan Shelley.*

[1]In August 1940 the name Home Guard was introduced.

Of course when it came to the question of arming the Home Guard there was a great problem of what to arm them with. Territorial units had most of the serviceable rifles – many of these were to be left behind after the Dunkirk disaster – so Home Guard commanding officers had to resort to scraping the bottom of a very nearly empty barrel. British police authorities, unlike those of our American or Continental cousins, had always frowned on private individuals keeping lethal firearms and ammunition around the home, so even before World War II legislation regarding the ownership of pistols and rifles had been strictly enforced. In 1941 even steel pikes had been issued to certain Home Guard units to become known, rather cynically, as 'Lord Croft's Pikers' after the junior minister who had been instrumental in issuing them. For years after they became almost a music-hall joke and even today still bring a smile to the lips of those old enough to remember. How reminiscent of a bygone age when we read in the *Ipswich Journal* for 1803: 'St Osyth Volunteers Commanded by Frederick Nassau Esq. stack their pikes in the gatehouse of St Osyth Priory.'

Weapons were desperately needed, so much so that a nationwide appeal was launched in an attempt to procure arms. From museums and private collections around East Anglia we find reports of many fine, old, valuable weapons being handed in to Home Guard commanders. As already mentioned, a great number were muzzle-loaders and the chance of finding proper-size balls or, even more important, powder, flint or percussion caps to discharge the pieces was slender. Enterprising members of the Home Guard who could add a little poaching to their many other strange and sometimes illegal talents, improvised fire-power with all sorts of volatile mixtures. One commander at Gestingthorpe – whilst experimenting with home-made explosives – succeeded in blowing himself and five of his men to pieces, and near Bury St Edmunds an early bronze Chinese cannon was shattered into a thousand fragments when loaded with an unstable mixture.

Things certainly improved later in the year when the Americans shipped over half a million World War I surplus rifles and bayonets, and soon afterwards discipline took a turn for the better. No longer did lone patrols spring from hedges and ditches at random to hold frightened waggoners or district nurses at bay with a shotgun. Now, civilians who didn't stop on command at a check point manned by Home Guard sentries stood the chance of being shot for now they had the power to stop and request a show of identity cards.

One of the greatest scares prevalent during those early days was that of enemy paratroopers. Not only were they reckoned to be lurking behind every other tree, bush or pillar-box, but they adopted all sorts of disguises. Nuns and postmen were the favourite and many were the poor old postmen who found themselves marched off to the police station just because a wary Home Guard had become over-diligent and suspicious. Wild and woolly were the number of rumours and tales relating to what one was likely to encounter when a group of *Fallschirmtruppen* drifted down from the skies. One tale, which even today is still spun around the wild-fowling Fens district, tells of how you couldn't bring down a German parachutist with ordinary bullets or shot. Just like the legendary Black Forest werewolf who could only be dispatched with a silver bullet, so too did you have to kill the enemy with a special load. Just how this rumour came into being we shall never know but it probably stems from the fact that the War Office, at about that time, had issued a special ball-cartridge for use against descending enemy paratroopers.

Foreign observers failed to be suitably impressed with the turnout and drill of those early LDV/HG members, for without uniforms they seemed to be a proper rag-a-tag bob-tail lot altogether. In fact in some instances the only distinguishing feature they boasted was the LDV armband which had hastily been run-up by local members of the WVS. Hundreds of these khaki brassards had been manufactured and distributed by the hard-pressed women who worked around the clock in shifts to complete their allotted task.

Self-appointed officers tended to sport golfing, hacking or cycling outfits; although it was reported in one Essex garrison town that a couple of gentlemen had turned up on parade dressed in gorgeous scarlet and blue uniforms weighed down with orders and medals and complete with a General Officer's ivory hilted sword, relics indeed of the old Indian Empire. Other ranks – if at all lucky – sported moth-eaten forage or side caps left over from the Great War.

William Joyce – or Lord Haw-Haw, to give him the title by which thousands of British listeners knew him so well – had a field day over the Home Guard. He delighted his vast audience with snippets of intimate and at the same time interesting information. Although the authorities frowned on those listening-in to his witty, pithy obser-vations; for sometimes he came so very near the truth – they never forbade anyone to tune into station Bremen at around 9 o'clock every evening . . . what is the old saying? 'We always want the things which are forbidden to us, and desire those which are refused'.

On the subject of the Home Guard, he tried to dissuade volunteers from joining the force by darkly hinting that if they were caught bearing arms they were liable to be shot as *franc-tireurs*. He said: 'Suicide academies have apparently been set up all over Britain. The headmasters are cunning blackguards who teach their inmates how to make bombs at the modest cost of two shillings each, how to poison water supplies by throwing dead dogs into streams and how to kill sentries noiselessly from behind: . . . Truly the Lord has afflicted these people with blindness!'

Training schools had indeed been set up, one of the most famous being at Osterley Park in Middlesex. Privately financed by a group of wealthy anti-Nazi industrialists[1], the school was run by Tom Wintringham, a former active Communist who had practised his skills whilst commanding the British contingent in the International Brigade – a left-wing faction that fought during the Spanish Civil War. During the 'phoney war' period Wintringham had also helped to launch a do-it-yourself assassins programme for civilians with numerous articles in magazines and newspapers.

Members of the Home Guard on the march 'Somewhere in England'.

[1]*The People's War.* Angus Calder.

At Osterley volunteers were taught how to kill and maim with just about anything that came to hand. Tanks could be knocked out with flaming 'Molotov cocktails'; a concoction of petrol, tar and paraffin packed judiciously into any size glass bottle. Motor cyclists could be decapitated with a length of fine wire stretched across a roadway, while the fairer sex could play their part by leading lone unsuspecting enemy soldiers into shady spots to be quickly dispatched by a waiting accomplice.

In East Anglia, Home Guard units patrolled coastal and back-water areas and in lonely country districts they guarded railway bridges and electrical sub-stations. Factories formed their own Home Guard detachments while at Marconi Ltd. (the famous wireless communications people of Chelmsford) Home Guard members manned the light AA guns mounted around the factory grounds.

Other work carried out by members of the Home Guard included building defences and road blocks using anything that came their way – farm carts loaded with logs and masonry, steam-driven tractors, old cars and even brass-bedsteads stood ready and waiting by the roadside to be pushed into the path of the invading Germany army. Removal of sign posts and street names left newly arrived army personnel and 'townies' completely in the dark, necessitating the introduction of home-made signs which sported such announcements as 'To the Pub', 'To Town', or to 'HQ'. Ancient mile stones were uprooted and buried at random, many to be lost for ever. Those that proved too heavy or stubborn to shift were defaced alongside the war memorials. Those railways stations situated twenty miles from a coastal area saw the removal of name plates, while elsewhere only small name boards were allowed, having letters no more than three inches high.

Summer and autumn of 1940 was to see the introduction of a highly secret underground Home Guard guerilla movement . . . something entirely new in the realms of British defensive warfare . . . new, that is, if you discount our ancient British forebears who carried out guerilla-type raids on conquering Roman and Norman invaders. The authorities, having weighed up the situation and evaluated the lessons so painfully learned during the invasion of Europe, had very wisely decided that whatever happened, once the might of the German invasion had been launched, no amount of road barricades, concealed pits with bottoms sprinkled with sharpened stakes, or platoons of cutlass-swinging or knife-throwing fanatics,

34

could ever hope to hold off a well-trained enemy for long. It was decided to form some twenty odd 'Auxiliary Units' which were to include a smattering of army officers and 'cells' of Home Guard formed into guerilla bands[1]. Their job was to take cover once the invasion had been successfully carried out, only coming out of hiding once the bulk of the enemy had moved on, leaving a small occupation force installed in village or town. Then they would go to work. . .

In East Anglia it was left to Colonel Colin Gubbins to build a series of blocks or cells with men who knew the landscape, were conversant with wind and tide and, most important of all, could keep a still tongue in their heads. One such man was Roger Weeley – known locally as the Squire of Weeley – his family were no strangers to the work of militiamen for one of his ancestors had been instrumental in raising the local band of volunteers during the Napoleonic Wars. Originally 'Squire' (as he is called by the locals) Weeley had been approached by a childhood friend who had just returned from the evacuation of Norway.

'Telephoning me one early morning he enquired if I would take on an important job. It required six men who not only knew the land and marshes from Brightlingsea to Harwich but were men who could keep their mouths shut. He didn't mind what sort of past criminal records they'd got just so long as I could trust 'em'.

Among his villagers the 'Squire' knew just where he could lay hands on six such likely lads and soon their training was under way.

'One evening we had quite an interesting little exercise, for Brigadier Stanyer wanted us to help test his famous Stanyer Line tank trap which was built across the back of Harwich. A lot of extra troops had been brought into the area to defend the line and we were supposed to infiltrate through the defenders without being observed. Dressed in battle-dress overalls with faces painted black and armed with daggers, coshes, semi-automatic pistols and hand grenades, we caused quite a stir. Not only did we get through the defences unobserved, but we took a fair bit of ammunition from anti-aircraft and searchlight positions. This caused a certain amount of chaos'.

Of course security was of the utmost importance for, apart from the half-dozen men in each group or cell, nobody knew the identity of the men that made up other guerilla groups in the district. Important messages and orders were dispatched by several methods. In one instance a stile support-post had been hollowed out so that it was just large enough to hold a small cocoa tin. Concealed beneath a matching piece of rustic, well-weathered timber the tin was fre-

[1]*Invasion 1940.* P. Fleming.

quently used as a postbox. The Weeley guerilla movement used a drainpipe for their 'letter box', which was situated beneath a railway bridge at Frating. Messages that were 'posted' there were picked up by an unknown person . . . his identity remaining a complete mystery even up to the present time.

Membership of the 202 Battalion – as the underground army was officially called – asked for volunteers to live off the land and hide-up wherever they could find shelter. Intricate plans were evolved so that, once an enemy had landed, the men of 202 Battalion would not fight alongside other members of the Home Guard but slip away to previously built hiding-places to await the call to action.

Explosives in the form of gelignite, phosphorous bombs, detonators and hand-grenades lay buried in convenient places along their

Artist's impression of a Home Guard underground bunker built in Weeley Woods, Essex, during 1939-40.

Artist's impression of a one-man hide-hole constructed beneath a cattle-trough and used by members of the Home Guard underground unit.

route. In an area known as 'Weeley Woods' Roger Weeley built a brick, concrete and steel bunker deep in the side of a small hillock. From the outside it resembled an ancient barrow complete with a selection of wild overgrown bushes and trees. Inside, the brick-lined shelter had all the comforts of home. With bunk beds and enough food and supplies to support six men for a month or more, it was all a group of underground fighters could ever wish for. One last final touch was the ventilation shaft very cleverly built up through the centre of a thick bush. From the outside one would have suspected nothing.

One thing the men emphatically refused to do was sleep alongside unstable phosphorous bombs or gelignite . . . these being tucked away in waterproof holes *outside* the bunker.

Of course, once the enemy had landed and the guerilla bands had started to fight back, hostages could and would have been taken. It takes a very fanatical or downright callous sort of man to see members of his family put against the wall and shot without revealing the identity or whereabouts of his comrades. To counteract such an eventuality taking place with members of the 202 Battalion, men were forbidden to carry family photographs or letters likely to link them with a nearby town or village.

A number of hair-raising escapades took place involving members of this underground army. Most of them concerned the handling of explosives or unfamiliar foreign firearms. At one time a raw recruit was to report to his sergeant armed with a muzzle-loading Brown Bess flintlock musket circa 1803 vintage. He complained that although he had managed to find a lump of flint to jam between the jaws of the cock and had ground down enough red match heads for priming powder he could still not get the awkward thing to spit out the lump of lead he'd rammed down the barrel. When asked the leading question . . . 'What amount of black powder did you pour down the barrel?' he replied: 'I couldn't find any powder so I put in about three inches of cordite instead!'

One Anglian commanding officer hit upon the novel idea of using the floor of his public bar as a miniature rifle range. Arming his men with a selection of air-rifles 'liberated' from a closed amusement arcade, they popped away at empty beer bottles perched on stools at the end of the bar.

Storing of explosives always proved a problem and caches of highly dangerous nitro-glycerine or detonators were sometimes hidden in milk churns buried deep in the ground. Sometimes they lay there for years, completely forgotten. Such was the case a few years ago when it was suddenly announced in an Anglian paper that a wood in the Tendring district was being cleared to make way for a proposed housing estate. One former member of the 202 Battalion remembered that about six milk churns of nitro had been buried in that particular wood and contacted the authorities. Royal Engineers, with the aid of mine detectors, eventually discovered the hoard and found the leaking contents to be in a very unstable condition. Quite a large area had to be cleared and a great number of folk evacuated before the R.E.s dispatched the lot in one big bang.

Another case involving sticks of explosives buried around the footings of a railway bridge lay undiscovered until the mid-1960s. Every day for the past thirty years or more trains had trundled back and forth overhead just a few yards away from the lethal charges.

Even such dangerous escapades had their funnier sides. A pig farmer decided that one of the safest places to bury a parcel of ½lb sticks of black plastic explosive would be in a pig pen where a pregnant sow was confined. He reckoned that no German would risk searching that spot. One day as he passed by the pen, he happened to notice his fat old girl comfortably tucked up in a corner chewing on a long, black something. 'She looked for all the world like a Winston Churchill chewing on one of his big cigars!' mused the farmer. That 'something' turned out to be one of the sticks of explosive. Not counting on the rooting habits of swine when he had first thought of burying them in that pen, our farmer friend found that at least two or three sticks had ended up in the tum of Mrs Penelope Pig!

Another aspect of all the secrecy surrounding the underground army was trying to perpetuate a series of feasible stories to tell family and friends. Very often men of the guerilla movement had to contend with an awful lot of leg-pulling from members of the more orthodox Home Guard units. 'Just what did those blokes get up to night after night? . . . They most certainly didn't take part in the normal Home Guard activities, that's for sure.' One poor chap led an absolute dog's life when he was at home for his wife truly thought that he had a fancy woman tucked away in the next village. She refused to let him sleep in the same bed with her and it was not until long after the war had ended, when the man's commanding officer eventually explained to her just what he had been up to all those years, that she finally believed his story.

Stories of endurance, privation and even sheer stupidity . . . how about the Essex Home Guard officer who had a regular soldier on strength just to feed a flock (if that's the right word!) of carrier pigeons which were housed in a loft over his public house. The master plan was that, once the invasion alarm – code name CROMWELL – had been given this soldier would drape his waiting motorcycle with baskets of birds and make off at top speed towards London letting out his message-bearing birds along the way. In theory, perhaps, a very good idea but one important thing had been overlooked. The birds in question had only been trained to fly back to their pub-bound loft and not towards the smoke and grime of London town! . . . all vie with each other to forge the history of the Home Guard in East Anglia. In the beginning the whole organisation was run along the lines of complete and utter chaos but by the time of the great stand-down in September 1944 the H.G. soldiers who manned A.A. and search-light batteries could be counted alongside the rest of Great Britain's fighting forces. Flotsam and jetsam had been drastically weeded out during the early days, leaving a hundred and forty thousand[1] well-trained men to guard our island shores.

[1]Total strength of Home Guard in Great Britain 1944.

CHAPTER THREE

WOMEN AT WAR

Whoever said that a woman's place was in the home could have never been thinking of a nation at war with its back to the wall. Study the past record of that fair sex when faced with an adversary of unknown strength and one will soon find that woman is surely a creature to be reckoned with once aroused. In ancient times battalions of warrior women could be seen garbed in burnished armour fighting alongside their menfolk. Even up to the Napoleonic Wars wives accompanied husbands aboard British men-of-war, not only caring for their spouses but actually helping man the guns when under fire. A woman, Jane Townshend, serving aboard HMS *Defiance* at the Battle of Trafalgar, actually claimed and was awarded the Naval General Service medal and bar for that battle. *The Gazette* directed that all engaged at this action should be eligible for a medal 'without any restrictions as to sex'[1]. However, male chauvinism being what it

Women munition workers at Elliott & Garrood Ltd., Beccles, World War II, varnishing 20-pound mortar bombs. *Elliott Collection.*

[1]*Collector's Guide to Militaria.* D.E. Johnson.

was during that day and age, poor Jane didn't receive her award. On the Admiralty Medal Rolls we find the handwritten entry against her name 'upon further consideration this cannot be allowed'.

During the Crimean War brave, dedicated souls such as Florence Nightingale and her band of nursing sisters succoured and tended the wounded in the field, thereby establishing a criterion in the world of nursing. However, this was in fact but the thin edge of the wedge for it was to be well into the First World War before women really came into the foreground once again, donning the arms and armour of the twentieth century.

Back in World War I it was to be 1917 before women were taken onto the land, but during the 1939-45 conflict some 4,544 land girls were in employment by December of 1939. By the end of 1944 this figure had mushroomed to 80,000; East Anglia boasting 8,336 of these girls.

Women were at last throwing off the domestic yoke which had kept the majority of their sex chained to a kitchen sink and nursery for generations past. That first year of the war was to see over 43,000 girls serving in Women's Auxiliary Services in the Women's Royal Naval Service (Wrens), Auxiliary Territorial Service (ATS), Women's Auxiliary Air Force (Waaf's) and various nursing services. They maintained switchboards, cooked, drove vehicles and were even responsible for loading and arming AA guns along coastal batteries.

By early autumn of 1943 some hundred thousand women were working on the railways, serving and trained in nearly 250 different railway grades including such diverse tasks as sailmakers (sewing canvas sheets which covered open trucks), concrete workers, assistant architects, fitters, electricians, boiler cleaners, weigh-bridge workers, painters, lock keepers, blacksmiths and even stablemen.

In other fields they turned their hand to almost anything; milk girls, window cleaners, clippies, firewomen, engineering and munition workers.

Engineering was to prove the most popular of feminine wartime occupations for by January 1944 there were over 1,500,000 women employed in this particular work, earning an average of £3.10s a week.

At Royal Ordnance Factories women played an important part in handling and making explosives just as they had during the Great War, but the Second World War saw more strict security measures enforced among the workers. During World War I a number of munition workers had been killed by explosions due to sheer carelessness but now, before entering a magazine, the girls had to visit a special changing room. In here they changed into rubber-soled shoes, donned fire-proof magazine suits and turbans and applied special cream to face and hands to protect the skin from absorbing explosive powders. They were searched before-hand to ensure that any inflammable or abrasive substances such as keys, metal combs, lighters, hair grips, matches or nail files were not taken into the danger zone.

It was, in the main, such strict precautions as these that brought about a complete change in women's fashions. Wearing gas masks and steel helmets also brought about rapid changes in women's hair styles. Long hair and page boy cuts, a vogue so very popular just prior to hostilities, quickly succumbed to short, easily manageable styles. Factory workers set a fashion for headscarfs and turbans.

East Anglia, being largely devoted to agriculture, witnessed the first great influx of members of the Women's Land Army.

This unique force, whose ranks were made up of girls from all walks of life ranging from shop girls to private secretaries, typists and even ladies of the streets, was part of the Ministry of Agriculture and Fisheries but run and staffed entirely by women. The Hon. Director of W.L.A. was Lady Denman D.B.E. who not only devoted all her waking hours to the cause but also gave over her own home, Balcombe Place, as general H.Q.

On joining the W.L.A. every girl was supplied with two green jerseys, two pairs of breeches, two overall coats, two pairs dungarees, 6 pairs of stockings, three shirts, one pair of ankle boots, one pair of shoes, one pair of gum boots or boots with leggings, one hat, one overcoat with shoulder titles, one oilskin or mackintosh, two towels, an oilskin sou'-wester, a green armlet, and a metal badge. After every six months of satisfactory service she received a half-diamond cloth badge which was sewn on the armlet: after two years service a special armlet, and a scarlet armlet to replace the two year one after four years service.

Not only did the girls have to work on hedges, haymaking, harvesting, threshing and thatching but they also had to learn to cope with gas or shell-shocked farm animals. In the early part of the war with the frightening prospects of imminent gas warfare, instructions were issued on how to handle such an attack. A supply of sacks and cloths had to be kept dampened and laid over chicken coops, kennels and cowshed windows. If fields had been sprayed with lewisite or mustard gas it was the farmer's (and W.L.A.) duty to lead the injured and blistered cattle to decontamination areas, rubbing them down with a mixture of petrol and paraffin, bathing their eyes with a solution of bicarbonate of soda and anointing any sores with a bleach ointment. Horses had to have a bandage soaked in their own urine tied over their eyes while it was advised that feedbags should be issued during an attack filled with wet bran. For shock the old time favourite of watered brandy or whisky plus plenty of warm wraps could not be surpassed. Gas attacks fortunately did not materialize but the W.L.A. worked hard on practice runs and would indeed have been fully prepared for the worst.

Many of the girls learned to plough and during the 'Dig for Victory' drive wrestled with heavy tractors, ploughing late into the night aided only by a lantern hidden in a ditch or a lamp of low power tied to the plough. Before an order was introduced by the authorities allowing dimmed headlights on night-driven tractors a number of East Anglian farmers faced prosecution for contravening the black-out regulations.

For those girls who successfully managed to drive a tractor, special courses were introduced on servicing their iron steeds. However, certain tricks of the trade just could not be picked up during early training. Farmers who had to enter a report on the progress of of their charges noted that many of the girls had little knowledge of servicing a tractor. When asked how they left their tractors after work in winter, several replied; 'Oh, we just put them away in a shed with a cloth over them and go home.' They should have replied: 'We drain the radiator with its head down-hill, unscrew the radiator cap to prevent freezing on, and cover the engine with a rug or sack, and of course we leave it on paraffin not on petrol.'[1]

In fair weather or foul, girls of W.L.A. worked to grow food for the country. For those workers of eighteen years of age or over they would receive 22/6d for a forty-eight hour week (in summer it could be fifty or more hours).

Dig for Victory became a major project and around country districts posters stating 'Plough Now! by day and night,' flourished on the walls of public houses or on church notice boards. Thousands of acres of parkland, village greens and even that most hallowed of all hallowed English institutions, the cricket pitch, were given over to growing potatoes, sugar beet and other root vegetables. Not all farmers took kindly to being ordered to plough this or that field and to grow certain types of crops, for they reckoned they knew the land slightly better than a batch of 'college-based agricultural com-

[1]*The Women's Land Army.* V. Sackville-West.

mittees'. Land girls were, in fact, employed in labour gangs working under the control of the County War Agricultural Executive Committees which supervised local executives of the government's agricultural policies, much to the disgust of certain farmers.

As Mr Lloyd George was to stress when broadcasting to the nation about the land problem in some districts: 'To ask land to do its duty when it needs drainage is like asking a sick man to do a full day's work. The land is in ill-health. The blood in its veins is sour. The land is suffering from pernicious anaemia.'

How right he was for places like Suffolk did prove something of a problem to the agricultural authorities, for well over 40,000 acres of once productive soil lay overgrown with weeds and wild hedges. Given over to game preservations – a legacy of King Edward VII – a vast number of farms lay derelict, their roofs patched with tarred paper and sacking: they were, in fact, nothing better than East Anglian hill-billy hovels. Once underway, however, the war agricultural committees worked wonders, with the air over Suffolk hanging blue with clouds of smoke as acres of choking weeds and bushes were swallowed up by hungry fire. Later, with the advent of enemy night bombing raids, the lighting of bonfires was prohibited in any shape or form and even carcasses of cattle laid low with foot-and-mouth disease could no longer be destroyed by continual burning fires; instead they had to be buried in deep pits.

In Cambridgeshire the fens also proved a challenge and had the Land Girls digging for submerged, almost fossilized oak trees; relics of a bygone age when vast forests flourished about that area. In some instances the buried trunks had to be blown up by sappers, leaving the girls to tidy up the debris. At Nazeing, Essex, part of the rough common land was reclaimed by W.L.A. girls operating giant diggers; the land then being prepared to take barley, wheat and root crops.

Other tasks undertaken by W.L.A. were those of Timber Corps and Rat Catchers. Pit props were the outcome of the former while the latter, armed with long-handled spoons and tins of Arsenic and Zinc-phosphide, waged war on the rodent enemy. Over a thousand girls volunteered for the job and it was reported at the time that the animal skill displayed by the girls was widely appreciated by all except the victims. They trained for the main part in county centres, being instructed in the whole complicated science from the old fashioned method of working with traps or terriers to more up-to-date methods of poison and gas.

It was envisaged that once the war was successfully concluded, land girls would still be needed to build up the nation's food stock. Therefore husbandry proficiency tests, with examinations both oral and practical, in the following branches of land work were introduced:

Milking and dairy work. General farmwork. Poultry.
Tractor driving. Outside garden and glasshouse work.
Fruit work. Pest destruction.

Once these were passed she could progress to a forewoman's course which included:

Hoeing and singling mangolds, and setting gangs to work.
Shocking and tying sheaves, and setting gangs to work.
Haymaking and rick building plus thatching.
Cleaning with bagging hooks.
Using handbill and slasher on hedges, and laying a hedge.
Using pick and shovel and laying drain pipes.
Digging a post-hole, and fencing.
Using a brake, grooming and harnessing a horse.
Wet day jobs of sawing wood with various saws, making thatching pegs.
Sharpening tools and care of tools.

Just how successful these proved to be can be surely witnessed by the number of ex-land girls marrying East Anglian farmers. I wonder how many of them remember the words and music of their very own song which was bellowed out with gusto during harvest time. I have only included the official words:

BACK TO THE LAND

Back to the Land, we must all lend a hand,
To the farms and the fields we must go.
There's a job to be done,
Though we can't fire a gun
We can still do our bit with the hoe.
When your muscles are strong
You will soon get along,
And you'll think that a country life's grand.
We're all needed now,
We must all speed the plough,
So come with us – Back to the Land.

If World War I East Anglian land girls had worked hard then so too did their sisters of World War II, for with greater mechanisation

opening up vast areas of waste land, far more produce was grown
calling for longer, harder working hours. Around the coastal counties
of Norfolk, Suffolk and Essex, members of W.L.A. braved air
attacks to carry out their allotted tasks. It was a common sight to
witness a girl driving tractor and plough, tin helmet perched at a
rakish angle, while a rip-roaring dog-fight was going on in the skies
above her head. These girls not only worked on the land during those
troubled times but very often helped pull airmen from blazing crashed
aircraft and extinguished blazing ricks and barns set on fire by
incendiary bombs.

A great number of important jobs were undertaken by women and
around the airbases of East Anglia new aircraft were delivered by
women of the Air Transport Auxiliary. Formed in 1939 by a number
of experienced pilots who were ineligible for service with the RAF,
they used to ferry aircraft from factories to RAF aerodromes. In
1940 just eight women pilots had been admitted into the ATA but by
late 1944 there were over 100 women pilots and 900 ground crew.
They delivered fighters, twin-engined aircraft, and one or two pilots
specialised in ferrying four-engined bombers.

It was not only the officially organised bodies of women who
devoted time and energy to the local war effort. In Norwich a lone
housewife, Mrs Ruth Hardy, became organiser of a group calling
themselves 'Mutual Aid Good Neighbours Association'. The body
was planned along the lines of the ARP and an appeal was launched
for 2,000 street organisers, eighty post organisers, twelve group
leaders, and three divisional heads[1]. The prime aim of MAGNA was
to try and save the lives of people suffering from the effects of shell or
bomb shock. They offered shelter, sympathy and understanding, and
most important of all, warmth. Members of this organisation raised
funds by running dances, concerts and whist drives. Over 30,000
Norwich women joined MAGNA and around the city one could
observe a number of small yellow posters announcing the welcome
message that a 'good neighbour lives here'.

For nursing sisters the war was to prove a very trying time. Not
only did they have to contend with normal, everyday accidents and
emergencies but also with victims of bombing raids as well as a
steady influx of injured firemen, ARP and CD workers, plus
wounded survivors of ditched aircraft. Many of them worked around
the clock with hardly a break for sleep or refreshments during those
early days of the war.

One nurse, Dorothy M. Gregory, a resident of Billericay Hospital,

[1]*Norwich at War.* Joan Banger.

recalls one particular day during the Battle of Britain when the sky over their hospital literally rained parachutes. Two of these she remembers well for both fell to earth a mass of flames. One, a young pilot, died on the stretcher as he was brought into the ward. Whilst cutting off the burnt uniform, Nurse Gregory managed to save part of the Luftwaffe insignia which she kept for a number of years. The other badly burned airman, a British pilot, was lucky enough to survive his terrible injuries although for a number of weeks his life swung in the balance. His wife refused to leave his bedside and tended him daily, changing his dressings and seeing to his needs.

No story of the war would indeed be complete without mentioning the exploits of those Women in Green, the W.V.S. Wherever trouble or an emergency situation arose one could always be sure that somewhere, somehow, a member of that unique volunteer service would turn up with practical advice and comfort.

The Women's Volunteer Service had been first thought of during the spring of 1938 when the Home Secretary, Sir Samuel Hoare, had contacted the Dowager Marchioness of Reading with the idea of forming an organisation which could recruit women into the ARP. The aims of the organisation were to be:

(a) To stimulate the enrolment of women in the ARP services so as to bring the number of women in those services up to mobilisation strength as soon as possible.

(b) To bring home to all women, especially women in the household, what air-raids mean and what they can do for their families and for themselves.[1]

During those early days when practical exercises for wardens were often accompanied by sounds of falling and exploding bomb noises amplified over a gramophone, it was common practice, when women attended lectures, to modify the explosions to a 'soft bang' lest they upset them. Males still tended to think that the opposite sex was made of fine bone china and should be treated as such! How they soon changed their way of thinking once they saw those tough pieces of 'Royal Doulton' in action.

Volunteers were trained to drive cars and trucks and also carry out their own maintenance. Driving in black-out was a hazardous enough occupation for an advanced driver let alone for women who up to the war had perhaps, if they were lucky, driven only in fine weather for a day's outing or shopping spree. To accustom them to cope with black-out driving, a special course in driving without lights was

[1]*Women in Green.* C. Graves.

introduced. Drivers steering without even the assistance of side-lights manoeuvred their bulky and unfamiliar vehicles around mattresses stuffed with straw which had been laid in their path to simulate dead and injured victims of a bomb attack. When this phase of their training had been completed, drivers practised driving while wearing gasmasks. At that early stage of the uneasy peace everything, including evacuation plans, was classed as top secret.

Just how popular the idea of the WVS organisation became speaks for itself, for by the end of 1938 volunteers numbered 32,329.

The distinctive WVS uniform which soon became as familiar as those worn by the ARP, Police or CD was evolved because, as Lady Reading so rightly argued, women who were uncomfortable about their personal appearance could not be expected to work in unison with other, perhaps better dressed companions. Jealously regarding clothes even in wartime could, and did, cause unnecessary friction.

The colour green was not a popular choice by any means but as khaki had already been selected by the ATS, brown by the Land Army, blue by the Waaf, and black by members of the Order of St John, green was the only suitable colour left. As so many people were superstitious about that shade it was decided, therefore, to weave a thread of grey into it. Beetroot red was used to trim jumper and hat and prevented a general air of drabness. Greatcoats were designed in such a manner that even if women slept in them overnight (as indeed many of them did!) it wouldn't show too much. Members were not given a uniform allowance; not only did they have to buy their own uniforms but also provide the clothing coupons.

And so the WVS was born. Their official birthday of 18 June coincided with the anniversary of the Battle of Waterloo and their slogan, which indeed they seemed to live by, was 'The WVS never says No'.

The Home Secretary was to say of this band of women: 'It is certain that in the event of war the calls upon the services of women will be many and urgent, and it is therefore important that they should be prepared. But I firmly believe that if this country can demonstrate to the world its capacity as a free community to organise itself for its own protection it will be one of the most effective ways of preserving peace.'

At first all women wanted to volunteer for ARP or First Aid Posts but the authorities had to impress upon them that those who served as clerks, cooks, laundry assistants, telephonists, stenographers and radiographers also played an important part in the war effort.

One of the major tasks undertaken by the WVS was to teach people the best way of how to jam wads of newspapers under their doors to prevent the infiltration of poison gas; how to fix babies' gas masks and teach women to cook for large numbers of people using makeshift and even outdoor cooking ranges. Other jobs entailed helping Service families. During the Baedeker raids on Norwich members of the WVS dealt with over 3,000 enquiries from Service personnel asking after the fate of their families. Gathering salvage, street and school collections for National Savings, making toys from scraps of timber, entertaining foreign airmen, even changing library books for hospital patients were also part of the job. When 'Wings for Victory', 'War Weapons', 'Warships' and 'Salute the Soldier' weeks came along it was the WVS who came to the fore to organise street and house-to-house collections.

The true testing point of this organisation was to be the evacuation. At most stages of the journey help was provided by the WVS. During the first three days of September 1939 a grand total of 1½ million people were evacuated. With the prospects of evacuation being completely alien to the British way of life, plans for this mass exodus of vulnerable civilians had to be gleaned and studied from other countries such as France, Germany and Spain who had suffered the pangs of mass evacuation during the 1914-18 and 1936-39 conflicts. Child-care under war conditions became part of WVS training and certificates were issued to volunteers who attained the approved standard. This also included working parties who altered clothing for needy children as well as supplying blankets and mattresses. When the bed-wetting problem reached astronomical proportions WVS members worked long stints filling canvas palliasse covers with straw. Blankets were made from every sort of material that they could lay hands on; tailors gave up their pattern books and bed-bound old ladies sewed them together alongside the age-old craft of knitting patch-work quilts. A vast quantity of the palliasse covers eventually filtered through from America and although they did in fact arrive too late for the evacuee problem they proved invaluable as sleeping bags, dust covers and covers for anti-shrapnel padding used on roofs of mobile canteens during the Blitz and Battle of Britain.

It was not only bedding that had to be improvised, for a nationwide appeal was launched to 'Make-do-and-Mend'. Materials which could be used for clothing for household linens were recovered from the most unusual sources. Special appeals were made for drawings on linen to be turned out by architects and engineers' offices; a very large number of these being boiled till the fine linen base was freed from the paper surface and could be used for children's clothes or hospital supplies. Flour bags were converted into tea cloths or shorts for local Cadet forces; the fabric used to cover broken windows and discarded by repair squads who reglazed them was washed until all the glue was removed, making excellent teacloths for re-housed bomb victims; old stockings were cut into strips and knitted into rugs; the little snippets left over from work-party premises were gathered up and stuffed into pillows for Rest Centres. In many rural districts children could be seen combing the hedgerows for hanks of sheeps' wool which was washed, spun and knitted by local housewives. Some areas resorted to a more novel form of wool collecting, taking the combings from suitable dogs, cats and even rabbits.

The WVS were also responsible for a national system of clothes dumps from which folk in need or distress could be kitted out within hours. Later a children's book, shoe and clothes exchange was introduced where mothers could take a youngster's outgrown garments or footwear and exchange it for a larger size.

Children and old folk played an important part in the duties of the WVS and when mothers of very young children began working *en masse* in factories and canteens, caring for the infants became a mammoth problem. WVS nursing centres sprang up all over the country with the American Red Cross generously contributing over £78,000 for the maintenance and equipment of over one hundred WVS War Nurseries. The first two of these were opened on 29 September 1940, just sixteen days after the idea had been first conceived.

Our American cousins also offered gifts of clothing and food to WVS units for distribution to blitz victims or the poor and needy, including a quarter of a million knitted sweaters, sixty thousand knitted woollen dresses and fifty thousand pairs of gumboots. Cases and boxes of all shapes and sizes flooded in from the States; in one month alone the value of goods received totalled £670,000.

One can only wonder just what age-group was attracted to the WVS and statistics[1] showed that the ARP Services appealed to single women between the age of thirty-five and forty while younger ones volunteered for Civil Nursing Reserve. Older women offered their services for hospital supplies; those too young to join the CNR enrolled as 'Junior WVS Hospital Helps'. A rather humorous anecdote is related of the woman who volunteered for the Civil Nursing Reserve and thought that her miniscule knowledge would be

[1]*Women in Green*, page 22

Above: Luftwaffe emblem cut from the tunic of a fatally burned fighter pilot shot down over Billericay during the Battle of Britain.

Left: A group of Field Ambulance Nursing Yeomanry (5th London Motor Coy.) shown here at Reed Hall Barracks, Colchester, 1941. Miss Peggy Oswald (now Mrs Sams), of Frinton-on-Sea, is demonstrating the use of a grease gun. Note the black-out hoods on the headlamp!

52

eagerly accepted. She was rather taken aback when, after being asked: 'Do you have any knowledge of bones?' and she replied 'Yes', found herself in charge of a WVS Salvage Station collecting, among other various items of scrap, old bones!

Food rationing certainly brought its problems and was always the uppermost thought in people's minds. For housewives trying to plan suitable meals for a young family the WVS held cookery demonstrations showing housewives how to tackle such strange dishes as whale meat, salted cod, fat bacon and that good old wartime standby, Spam. Later, street parties were held to demonstrate and popularise eating baked potatoes in their jackets.

In East Anglia during July 1941 the introduction of the famous Pie Scheme was launched. Introduced at Cambridge, the WVS organised the distribution of home-cooked pies to agricultural workers engaged in gathering the harvest. By delivering food direct to workers in the field, valuable time was saved as well as supplying much needed rations of food. Transport wasn't always of the more

The 'Pie Scheme'. A member of the WVS delivering pies to hungry farm workers during the Second World War.

conventional form and the food was often carried out into the fields in anything that came to hand; old prams, handcarts, baskets, and even the odd wheel-barrow.

The WVS also gave advice and demonstrations on how to cook a meal with the aid of sealed food containers and the hay box, one of the oldest methods of heating known to mankind.

Mobile canteens also visited AA and searchlight batteries, bringing a little cheer and comfort to the often isolated groups of men and women. At Spalding the local newspaper wrote of one WVS canteen driver who set out on a tour of Britain's bleakest marshes to visit the troops. They named her 'The Florence Nightingale of the Marshes'. Through dense fogs and in the black-out she drove her camouflaged van fifty miles a day for six days a week. Half of it was fitted up as a canteen for selling tea and cakes. The other half was equipped as a shop in which she sold all manner of goods ranging from birthday

Members of the WVS building emergency field kitchens from old tin boxes, bricks and clay. These were put to good use during the heavy bombing raids on Norwich.

cards to hair cream. The first fourteen weeks the vehicle travelled over 4,000 miles, during which period twenty thousand cups of tea and thirty-seven thousand cakes were sold.

Nearer the bigger towns there appeared the infamous British Restaurant in answer to people needing a cheap, hot mid-day meal. In districts laid low with heavy raids causing disruption of gas, water and electricity supplies, a special WVS Queen's Messenger Convoy was rushed to the area. Although mobile canteens could and did cope with minor raids it was decided by the Ministry of Food that some more powerful method of emergency feeding must be introduced. Q.M. convoys consisted of a dozen vehicles: two food storage lorries, two equipment lorries, four motor-cycles, one water-tank lorry, and three mobile canteens. A team of fifty volunteers staffed this convoy and apart from men driving the heavy lorries and shifting bulky kitchen equipment they were all women. This scheme eventually led to the formation of the Mobile Emergency Feeding Units equipped with a collapsible shed, furniture, solid fuel burner, store of fuel, water and food and important items of crockery.

A far more static arrangement was the introduction of the WVS hostel. One of these was opened in Cambridge for service women, also catering for wives and girl friends of servicemen stationed in the district. A special Polish hostel and canteen was also built in that ancient academic city, where a party of Polish ATS girls who had escaped from occupied Poland during the early part of the war found a most welcome home-like atmosphere in the form of books, English lessons and, most important of all to that Slavic race, music and song.

Some centres in the more rural parts of East Anglia purchased a number of bicycles which could be left at bus or railway stations so that stranded servicemen could borrow them to return to barracks in time for roll call.

Work carried out by WVS infiltrated to all levels and branches of British society. Wherever one looked during those six long, bitter years one could always be sure of catching sight of Women in Green. When the American President's wife Mrs Roosevelt paid a flying goodwill visit to our battered island late in the war she was shown, among many other things, an exhibition held at Cambridge demonstrating the type of work carried out by the WVS . . . bookbinding for Forces Mobile Library; making toys and dolls houses for nurseries; carpet slippers for Rest Centres; sniper suits, furniture for AA and searchlight huts and even leather jackets for minesweeper crews made from old scraps of leather. One of the hardest tasks undertaken was that of making the camouflage netting used to cover guns, tanks, and aircraft. With the coarse netting spread out the women crawled on hands and knees to weave in pieces of green, yellow and brown dyed scrim to form a loose-knit camouflage pattern. Altogether 129,558 nets were garnished by WVS for the Ministry of Supply.

Working in close harmony with the WVS was the National Federation of Women's Institute. This latter group was largely responsible for forming the Country Herb Committee set up by the Ministry of Supply in 1942 to organise the collection of medicinal herbs. In small villages W.I. members organised bands of local children to gather the bundles of nettles, foxgloves, raspberry leaves and rose hips. The youngsters were paid 1½d a bundle for the leaves and 3d a pound for rose hips and conkers. Something of a record was established that first year when over three and a half tons of conkers were collected at one depot. At Great Bentley, one of the sixteen packing stations in Essex, Mrs F. Atthill and Mrs A. Burgess prepared the bundles of leaves for dispatch by rail to the appropriate chemical works. The rose hips were made into syrup which was issued to mothers and young babies, while the conkers went to make tannic acid for creams and lotions so important in the treatment of burns. Preparing the bundles of leaves was a most exacting task calling for a lot of patience. In the drying centres around East Anglia one could often see trays of slowly drying leaves set out in rows under the hot sun but with unstable British weather a W.I. weather-guard was always on duty.

And so the women worked on. The men may have had the glory of fighting, dying and being maimed for their country but that old saying 'A woman's work is never done' was especially true during that period of Britain's history. Whether it was washing the bruised and bleeding feet of exhausted soldiers returning from the crushing defeat of Dunkirk or unravelling tops of old socks to be re-knitted into balaclava helmets or cap comforters, they slogged on not only with their work but with their normal everyday housework routine. It seems quite fitting that at the end of hostilities it should be a group of Anglian women who made a little history. On Sunday 13 May 1945 two German E-boats arrived at HMS *Beehive* (Felixstowe Docks) bringing Rear Admiral Karl Bruening, officer-in-command of E-boats operating from Dutch bases, and his advance party to arrange the surrender of his boats. He was piped aboard the Admiral's Barge (which was manned by Wrens) by a receiving party and given a smart salute by the coxswain, Leading Wren M. Cherrill.

CHAPTER FOUR

CIVVY STREET

One often reads accounts of how World War II affected the lives of service personnel with all the upheaval and privation that goes with service life, but of a civilian population who in the main were just as bewildered as the next person with all the hastily imposed regulations and restrictions, one hears very little.

For East Anglians the outbreak of the war was to prove no different to anywhere else in Great Britain but come the spring of 1940 and things soon began to move on to a war-footing with restrictions to personal liberty which are so alien to East Anglian natives.

The noise of a wailing siren is a mournful sound and one that the civilian population of Great Britain had to endure for six years. It was hard enough for humans to accept the noise but for thousands of pet animals it was something which was to bring fear and apprehension on a major scale. Our nation of pet-lovers recoiled in horror when it was first announced that animals were not to be allowed into the shelters no matter how they were handled. Mid-September 1939 was to see the wholesale slaughter of cats and dogs as people evacuated, enlisted or moved to safer parts of the country. Pets whose well-run lives had been regulated like clock-work, strolling in for meals with the family or curling up at the end of the day in a well-worn favourite chair, now fled in terror at the first sound of a siren. Sometimes they would run for miles until dropping from exhaustion; others hid in sheds or cellars for days on end. With their lives completely disorientated they wandered the streets until taken into care and final destruction. RSPCA figures for the first fortnight of the war list something like 200,000 dogs being destroyed. For those who didn't relish the thought of tying their pets to a fence or nearby lamp-post they could purchase from the PDSA a gas-proof kennel for £4. Likewise the pets of those with necessary funds could spend the war in the peace and tranquility of good old Donegal . . . cost being '£1 a week for gun dogs, others, 10/-'.

Alongside the list which was posted in frontroom windows letting CD or ARP authorities know how many people resided therein, another small ticket issued by the Canine Defence League told of the number of dogs one could expect to find if the premises were bombed.

About that time another scheme was introduced to save a soldier's dog or find a home for those dogs left behind without means of shelter.

If a dog was young or fit enough it could always join up! 'The RSPCA urgently requires more dogs for active service with the British Army. They are: . . . Alsations, Airedales, Lurchers, Collies and crosses between them, Bull Terriers, Elk Hounds, Himalayan Sheep Dogs, Rhodesian Ridge-Backs and Dutch Barge Dogs, being over 9 months old and under 6 years of age.'

In more rural parts of East Anglia this problem with pets didn't arise for as with generations past they roamed farmyards and small-holdings as they pleased, doing their job of keeping vermin at bay.

What was life like for those left at home after loved ones had answered the call to arms? With black-out, rationing and shortages in general, not very good it seems. The wife of a private soldier with two young children received twenty-five shillings a week plus seven shillings stopped from her husband's pay leaving him one shilling a day to purchase luxuries such as soap, cigarettes, sweets or a supper at the NAAFI. Almost from the beginning, restrictions in one form or another started to take over the civvy way of life. National Registration on 29 September 1939 was one major step in curtailing the personal liberty of the individual. Name, address and National Registration number were entered in a small blue folded card which had to be carried by the owner at all times. Failure to do so could result in a fine of two shillings as a young Norwich girl found to her cost. In October came introduction of ration books, but the first time to take them shopping was on Monday 8 January 1940 though only for ham or bacon, four ounces a head a week, butter four ounces, and sugar twelve ounces. Meat rationing started in March with 1/10d worth a week for those over the age of six, and 11d worth for smaller children; the adult ration eventually being reduced to 1/1d worth. In July, rationing proper was introduced when tea was rationed to just two ounces a week. For a tea-loving Britain what more could the authorities do? By the end of 1940 most family store cupboards were almost bare. Tins of preserves, dried fruits, biscuits, tinned fish, all had vanished from the shopkeepers' shelves and housewives took to spending hours queuing outside shops in the vain hope of buying just anything. One King's Lynn housewife recalls the time when she joined a queue outside a local shop, standing a good hour and a half until she reached the counter. Her purchase? A couple of fly papers! As she said: 'I didn't know what they were selling but thought if there's a queue it must be for something worthwhile! I bought them not because I needed them but only to justify the time spent queuing.' In a way this queuing became a British way of life . . . people queued for buses and trains, theatres, food, and even outside air-raid shelters.

Against an almost typically Orwellian 1984 backcloth, street hoardings, post offices and public shelters and transport sported Government posters extolling all manner of things to do or not to do. At one time there were no fewer than four dozen such works of art on display ranging from 'Not to Waste', 'Join the AFS', 'Save for Victory', 'Help build a 'plane' to 'Eat National Wholemeal Bread'. Magazines and newspapers also spent the war years bombarding the housewife with military style communiques. *Kitchen Front Communique No 7* tactfully advised that 'One well-warmed room in one house is more sensible (and much more comfortable) than two rather chilly rooms in separate houses . . . So don't delay – get together with your friends and neighbours now and work out a scheme for sharing firesides this winter'. People in towns did follow this plan and it became common practice for neighbours to bring a lump of coal along when asked out for the evening. During the bad winter of 1940 – the coldest winter for over forty years when rivers froze over and snow falls blocked road and rail traffic – fuel supplies hit an all-time low with folk trying to keep warm by burning all manner of strange things. For those folk living in country areas an afternoon walk now meant bringing home odd pieces of wood or a bag of fir cones to burn. For 'townies' old shoes stuffed tight with rolled-up newspaper and coaldust; coaldust mixed with wet cement and left to dry into egg-shaped briquettes; even sawdust mixed with scotch-glue resulting in a foul smelling crematorial glow; all contributed to bringing a little warmth to a depressingly cold war-bound Britain. The authorities tried to encourage householders to burn coke on their open fires which was obtainable from local gas works rationed to 28 lb per person. With a shortage of man-power there were no deliveries and one often saw queues of customers outside the gas works wheeling many odd-looking vehicles. Ancient prams (both doll's and children's), the odd sledge or two, Grandpa's basket-work bath chair and in one instance at Colchester, a knife-grinder's barrow. Even bombing raids had their compensations, for shattered timber was dragged from the bombed buildings to be dumped in a town centre where the inhabitants could fight among themselves for the best pieces. Towards the end of the winter it became common practice to sift the cold ashes for any remaining unburnt pieces of coal and coke to be press-ganged into a second round of burning.

Candles and torches vanished from the shops almost overnight as they were snapped up for use in shelters and blacked-out streets.

When they were obtainable the price had doubled and trebled. Soon folk began to catch on to little tricks and skills of the time. Torches which had to be dimmed when used in the streets could have their beams effectively reduced by inserting two or three discs of thin, white paper beneath the glass; batteries would last that little bit longer if removed from the torch during daylight hours and stored on top of a heater; to coax the last few rays from a fading battery running it up and down an occupied trouser-leg was supposed to work wonders.

For those lucky enough to own a bath sporting a hot water system yet another ruling was introduced: no more than five inches of bath water. In some cases the bath was marked with a black painted line five inches from the bottom.

Throughout the war the public were cajoled and bullied into accepting fresh restrictions and shortages. One leading daily newspaper ran a campaign asking everyone to breed rabbits to eke out the meat ration. They even issued instructions (for non-country types) on how to dispatch your fluffy friend.

'When a rabbit has to be killed the best method to be used by comparatively inexperienced people is as follows: The rabbit should be held by the hind legs and given a sharp blow at the nape of the neck with the edge of a flat piece of wood. The piece of wood should be about eighteen inches long by three inches wide and one inch in thickness, with the striking edge bluntly tapered. No great force is necessary in delivering the blow and death is instantaneous. After stunning, the throat should be severed.'

Later, it became practice to issue a wooden block with a 'V' cut in one side. This was screwed onto an outside wall near the kitchen; the neck of the bird or rabbit being slipped into the 'V' and with a quick downwards jerk the game was dispatched.

Clothes rationing was introduced on 1 June 1941 and with just a basic ration of forty-eight coupons a year many people let their standard of dress fall below par. In a broadcast to the nation by the President of the Board of Trade it was emphasised: 'I know all the women will look smart, but we men may look shabby. If we do we must not be ashamed. In war the term "battle-stained" is an honourable one.' Many men and women took to wearing siren suits . . . a one-piece garment made very much along the lines of a baby's romper suit having a long zip in the front and a pixie-type hood. Many folk wore these to sleep in when driven to the shelters by all-night bombing-raids, and Winston Churchill popularised them by wearing one when visiting bombed-out districts.

From June 1942 it was illegal to manufacture bedspreads or table-cloths and blankets and sheets became almost unobtainable except to those newly-weds or victims from bombings. Make-Do-and-Mend became a way of life for everybody. Flour sacks were washed, dyed and used as curtaining or blankets and with pieces of coloured rag threaded through with a sack-needle served as durable, though slightly rustic, floor covering. Oil cloth or linoleum also disappeared from the scene and around East Anglia it became the custom to utilise rolls of heavy-duty roofing felt, being painted with two or three coats of paint once firmly tacked to the floorboards.

Some idea of what clothes rationing meant can be gathered from a contemporary list issued as a guide to the trade.

MAY 1942, CLOTHING COUPONS

Men and Boys	Adults	Children
Unlined mackintosh or cape	9	7
Other mackintoshes, raincoat, overcoat	16	11
Coat, jacket, blazer, and like garments	13	8
Waistcoat, pullover, cardigan, jersey	5	3
Trousers (other than fustian or corduroy)	8	6
Fustian or corduroy trousers	5	5
Shorts	5	3
Overalls, dungarees, and like garments	6	4
Dressing-gown, bathing-gown, pair pyjamas	8	6
Shirt, combinations – woollen	8	6
Pants, vest, bathing-costume, child's blouse	4	2
Shirt, combinations – other material	5	4
Pair socks, or stockings	3	1
Collar, tie, or two handkerchiefs	1	1
Scarf, pair of gloves or mittens	2	2
Pair of slippers or galoshes	4	2
Pair of boots or shoes	7	3
Pair of leggings, gaiters, or spats	3	2

Women and Girls	Adults	Children
Coat, raincoat, lined mackintosh	14	11
Jacket, short coat	11	8
Dress, gown, frock – woollen	11	8
Dress, gown, frock – other material	7	5
Blouse, sports shirt, cardigan, jumper	5	3
Gym tunic, girl's skirt with bodice	8	6
Overalls, dungarees, and like garments	6	4
Skirt, divided skirt	7	5
Apron, pinafore	3	2
Pyjamas	8	6
Nightdress	6	5
Petticoat, slip, combinations, cami-knickers	4	3
Other undergarments including corsets	3	2
Pair of stockings	2	1
Pair of socks, collar, tie or two handkerchiefs	1	1
Scarf, pair of gloves or mittens, muff	2	2
Pair of slippers, boots, or shoes	5	3

Knitting wool, 2 ounces, required 1 coupon.

Later that year cigarettes, tobacco and even the humble match became short in supply. A utility cigarette was introduced to the British smoker known as 'Pashas'; a Turkish brand that smelt and tasted like roasted camel dung, or so a former Lowestoft policeman believed! One Frinton smoker was driven to the extreme measure of experimenting with chrysanthemum leaves. Drying flower and leaves in the range-oven he hand-rolled the results into foul-smelling cigarettes. During the war he was to try various leaves and plants. He swore by blackberry leaves and even rhubarb but confessed that chopped straw mixed with lavender and geranium leaves nearly killed him!

Soldiers cashed-in on the match shortage by utilising spent .303 rifle cartridges and making them into small, ornate cigarette lighters.

Table lighters were made from used cannon, mortar and Bofor shell cases, many bearing ornate scrimshaw work setting-out details of regimental histories, battle engagements or town names.

Drink was another commodity that became short in supply. The first war-time advertisement by the brewing industry announced cheerfully: 'Beer is best – it makes for contented workers, friendliness and tolerance, as the Government found out in the last war. Above all – beer makes for the British cheerfulness which is undefeatable. So stick to Beer.' This sentiment could have been accepted *if* supplies had held out but with the manpower shortage and basic ingredients many public houses were forced to introduce their own rationing scheme. The price of beer was to rise until by 1944 it was 1/3d a pint. Spirits were over 25/- a bottle and nearly four times that amount was in fact paid if and when a stray bottle could be tracked down. Many tried to brew their own, very often with disastrous results. On one Anglian airbase, coloured American servicemen supplied a nearby town's wants by manufacturing their own Scotch using a bizarre concoction which relied on high octane aircraft fuel for its kick. The team was completely organised even down to the labels and cap seals. It subsequently transpired that the leader had run a 'moonshine' still over in the States.

With so many shortages and luxury goods that age-old business of supply and demand came to the fore. In the main the general public grudgingly accepted the restrictions solely for the reason that they couldn't do anything but accept them. For those with influence or, better still, money, any rationed items or goods in short supply could be obtained at a price. Even normal, everyday household items were at a premium and anything secondhand was soon snapped up by an eager, waiting public . . . In an East Anglian newspaper for 1941 folk advertised their 'Wants' . . . the 'For Sale' column being almost empty. 'WANTED . . . Hoover cleaner, between £10-£12 paid for S/H model'. One little Clacton farm worker spent his leisure hours dragging abandoned bicycles from the hedgerows, cleaning and repairing them and selling them for £5-£6 each . . . almost a week's wages back in those days.

Although the organised black market was the work of a major crime syndicate a lot of lesser rackets were run on a local small-time basis. Shopkeepers drew supplies for phantom customers; small engineering firms drew government allowances and wages for non-existent war-workers. Ration books which in some cases had been left at a shop to save the trouble of dragging them back and forth each shopping trip were 'stolen', and for those with London contacts a supply of illegally forged and printed coupons could be purchased. A couple of war-time sayings summed it all up: 'Sorry! nothing in today – don't you know there's a war on?' and 'I bet he's got some under the counter!'

This war was to breed a type of character the likes of which had never been seen before . . . the spiv. Dressed in a loud suit, brown and white shoes, a long, wide garish necktie, padded shoulders and a snap-brimmed hat, the overall picture was completed by the wearer sporting a thin, pencilled moustache. Usually living on their wits and only just within the law, many of the spivs were service deserters and column dodgers. They acted as go-betweens in black market transactions, knowing when and where to lay hands on just about anything. Most large towns had them and in East Anglia they could often be seen in public houses or hotels clinching a shady deal with certain gentlemen farmers, market gardeners or American service-men.

It wasn't only in civvy street that black market activities flourished. In 1942, at a Colchester Court Martial, four officers of the Royal Army Service Corps were dismissed from the service for certain irregularities. These ranged from receiving coal and paraffin, improperly drawing servants' allowances, stealing food and permitting repairs to be done to private cars in an RASC workshop by soldiers and civilians. This was but the tip of the iceberg for rolls of barbed wire, field kitchens, timber, motor tyres and even type-writers vanished from stores to re-appear on the open market. In some cases whole crates of tinned food were stolen and buried in slit-trenches to be retrieved at a later date and sold to hotels, restaurants, or indeed anybody with ready cash and a still tongue.

One colourful character who assisted in the laying of heavy-duty searchlight cable along the clifftops of Harwich, Frinton and Walton kept a plan of the exact position of each stretch of cable, returning after the war to dig them up. Cutting it into handy size pieces he carted away several tons of the valuable copper wire ready to be sold as scrap when prices rose.

A lot of tales have circulated about various black market enterprises but one of the funniest must be the one concerning the antics of an East Anglian pig-swill man. This chap had a working understanding with a cook at one of the large army camps he visited daily to pick up swill. For an undisclosed sum the cook would leave among the kitchen waste a few choice off-ration items. Sometimes it was a tin of ham or perhaps a few tins of fruit, but whatever it was it was always smuggled out among the swill. A keen police inspector getting wind of the fiddle decided to catch the pair red-handed and sprang a vehicle check at the camp gates. Standing majestically in front of the evil-smelling load as it made to pass out of the camp the inspector ordered the entire load to be emptied out onto the driveway. Imagine his chagrin when after sorting through the highly perfumed heap he found nothing in the way of contraband at all, only potato peelings and fish heads. It must have been luck that on that particular day the cook had reported sick with a touch of food poisoning!

Petrol was another field in which black marketeers found a lucrative opening. Branded petrol, having been replaced by 'pool' at the beginning of the war, cost 1/6d a gallon rising to 2/1½d. On the black market one could pay 6/6d a gallon or more. Although petrol for commercial use was dyed bright red, it was but the work of a moment to remove this give-away dye by pouring the petrol through a gas mask filter or adding a small measure of Brobat bleach to the tank.

For those not prepared to deal with black market goods and who still tried to struggle on using their motor-cars, the idea of gas propulsion seemed an ideal solution. The Fuel Research Station and British Coal Utilisation Research Association advocated the use of gas, anthracite or coke, planning to set up a series of supply points at strategic positions around large towns. Gas was carried in a bag mounted on the car roof and with the aid of a special auxiliary carburettor could run for approximately twenty miles at one filling. Unlike World War I when the gas bag had a nasty habit of flopping down over the windscreen once empty, thus causing the motorist to drive blindly resulting in a number of accidents, the new version was encased in a bellows-like structure allowing the material to fold back into place as the bag emptied. The cost of this nine feet long, six feet wide and four feet high encumbrance which contained 202 cubic feet of town gas was £30 . . . that vast amount of gas only equalling a single gallon of petrol. Its life-span was very short for by October 1942 all further conversions had been banned due to a growing fuel shortage. Instead, commercial vehicles were equipped with a producer-gas generator towed behind the vehicle on a small trailer. The burner resembled a large dustbin on wheels and burned well over a ton of anthracite a week with frequent overhauls and maintenance to ensure a useful life. It was first introduced in East Anglia by a Mr M. Morrison who tried it out at Maldon on the Eastern National Bus Company. Although they acted as a form of fill-in until the petrol situation eased they did, however, suffer from prolonged teething troubles just like any other new invention. Passengers will no doubt remember them for their slowness and frequent calls to debus and push their transport up steep hills. Another unnerving experience was the problem of uneven surfaces which caused the burner to bounce about. At East Gates, Colchester, when passing over the level-crossing, red-hot coke would jump out of the burner catching light to the pitch-soaked, wooden road blocks; something of a hazard at night especially when a raid was on.

The number of cars left out in the road in 1940 (by today's standard) was relatively light but for all that they still made very good targets for marauding enemy hit-and-run fighters. In August 1940 the British Industrial Design Group suggested that private cars should be camouflaged, having one side of the vehicle painted to blend in with a hedgerow or brick wall. A number of garages had been appointed to apply this method of disguise at a cost of 35/- per car.

War creates many strange overtures and in turn even stranger bed-fellows. When Hitler attacked the USSR in June 1941 the British press were faced with something of a dilemma for up to that time the Bolsheviks had been tarred with the same brush as the Germans. In fact only a week before the invasion the 'dailys' had branded both Russians and Germans as evil twin sisters. Overnight they switched their tune, extolling the virtues of 'Our Russian Comrades in Arms'. Members of the left-wing Labour Party were overjoyed for now they could openly support their masters with new-found respectability. Even Mrs Churchill, that bluest of all true-blues, had a sudden change of heart, introducing her 'Fund for Russia' which raised over £8 million pounds for Britain's new-found ally.

Meanwhile, those who were injured by enemy action received help from the Assistance Board with grants for those folk who had temporarily lost their ability to earn a wage. A married man was allowed £1-5s a week while in hospital and £1-13s a week when he was discharged. He could claim 4/- a week for each of his first two children and 3/- a week for any addition to that number. Unmarried men could claim 11/- a week while in hospital and £1 a week when discharged while a single woman was allowed 9/6d a week while undergoing hospital treatment and 18/- a week when convalescent.

As air-raids continued to drive people away from the large towns so too did the population drop – people were not having families due to the split-up of the home or husbands posted overseas. In Norwich the population was to drop to 106,100.

With increasing privations the British public had little to laugh about during those early days. Entertainment, when available, was usually well below pre-war standards. Cinemas, apart from assailing the public with *Fuel Flashes, The Kitchen Front* and *Battle Orders* (a series of short films showing – among many other snippets of information – how a housewife should best poke her fire!) had programmes ranging from trite, third-rate American rubbish to the heavily sentimental British war-hero offerings. In East Anglia a great number of cinemas had been forced to close owing to the lack of audiences or Government restrictions but as troops began to move into de-populated areas and restrictions lifted, plate-glass doors swung open once again to welcome in eager audiences. Long queues waited in wind and rain to see such war-time epics as *Come on George* with George Formby, *The Murder in Thornton Square* with Charles Boyer and Ingrid Bergman, *Bulldog Drummond Strikes Back* with Ronald Colman and Loretta Young, and that tear-jerker of all tear-jerkers, *Goodbye, Mr Chips* starring Robert Donat. No longer was it possible to purchase sweets and ice-cream from the foyer for sweet-rationing was to clear the shelves overnight. Even the heating was down or non-existent and one soon got used to seeing patrons bringing blankets, hot-water bottles and even thermos flasks of soup or tea with them for their evening's entertainment. During air-raids it was the practice to flash on the screen a notice of the raid warning the audience to take to the shelter, but after a while it was only the faint-hearted who left the film. As one Walton resident remarked: 'We reckoned that if we were going to be hit then let's go while we were still enjoying ourselves'.

At home one could always listen to the gramophone or wireless to brighten up a dull day. As records were now in short supply, each large, fragile disc was treated with the utmost care. Dusted after each recital, it would be tucked away safely in its paper sleeve then packed away in a specially constructed cabinet. Young children no longer took turns to wind the machine up for if the spring was over-wound or damaged that would be the end of that, for any mechanical spares or repairs were a thing of the past.

On the wireless one could also listen to morale-boosting pro-grammes covering the *Kitchen Front* but lighter entertainment was served up in the form of various popular comedy programmes. Shows such as *Mind My Bike* with Jack Warner (Dixon of Dock Green fame), *Can you hear me Mother?* with Sandy Powell, *Band Wagon* with that ageless Arthur Askey and 'Stinker' Murdoch, and that inexhaustible concert organist Sandy Macpherson who on his *Sandy's Half Hour* programme received over 5,000 requests a week from service personnel and their families for request tunes to be played over the air. The most famous programme of all was to be *ITMA* (It's that Man Again) starring Tommy Handley, which piped out at 8.30 on a Thursday evening and brought to the listeners a comic masterpiece. In the beginning T.H. made his audience laugh at themselves as with his Minister of Aggravation and Mysteries hiding in the Office of Twerps, he quipped and joked with a number of odd characters . . . who will always be remembered with fond affection . . . such names as Funf, the German spy, or Mrs Mopp the bawdy charwoman who always entered with 'Can I do you now, sir?' and left with 'T.T.F.N.' (Ta ta, for now), a saying which even today is still used by that wartime generation. In close competition with *ITMA* was Lord Haw-Haw, with over a million British listeners tuning in to his wave-length every evening.

Haw-Haw, an Irish-American by birth, had decided to join the NSDAP cause in 1939 prior to the outbreak of hostilities. Formerly a member of Sir Oswald Mosley's British Union of Fascists he later broke away from the party to form his own National Socialist League. Once in Germany he became the chief broadcaster in English.[1] His nightly programme became very popular and by July 1940 the authorities had issued a press warning against listening to him.

'What do I do . . . if I come across German or Italian broadcasts when tuning my wireless? I say to myself: "Now this blighter wants me to listen to him. Am I going to do what he wants?" . . . I remember nobody can trust a word the Haw-Haws say, so just to make them waste their time, I switch 'em off or tune 'em out!'

One thing that war-time listeners remember about his broadcasts was his uncanny method of relaying intimate pieces of information about certain landmarks and supposedly top secret installations. He would tell his audience the night before when a certain target was to be bombed . . . even naming streets or Jewish-owned shops and factories that would receive those unwelcome night visitors.

Most of the songs written during that period usually carried morale-boosting messages either ridiculing the enemy or promising all manner of good times ahead *once* the war was won. Despite such good intentions, newspapers still gave reports of war-weary, worried people taking the only way out. Many of the suicides turned to the

[1]Captured after the war William Joyce stood trial and was executed as a traitor . . . erroneously as it transpired, for subsequent study of his documents revealed he had been an American at the time of his flight to Germany; America not entering the war until 1942.

sea, while others relied on gas, pills, the rope or railway lines. In the case of members of the armed forces they tended to rely on the pistol or rifle. In passing, it is interesting to note that once the invasion was launched in June 1944 the number of men going absent or deserting rose alarmingly. A Staff Officer serving on Court Martials at that time recalls that there was a marked increase of men being arrested suffering with self-inflicted wounds.

Songs best remembered from the war were ones like *Hang out the Washing on the Siegfried Line*; a song which sold over 200,000 copies during the first two weeks of publication. Another, rendered by the immortal Flannagan and Allan, was *Run Rabbit Run*, earning a small fortune for its authors and composer. One of its authors, Ralph Butler, originally heralded from Great Clacton, Essex.

There were good songs and there were bad, mediocre songs. One of the latter must surely be one reason those folk ended it all!

ONLY ONE OF THE TOYS

'I'm only one of the toys, my boy,
I do what I'm told to do,
Perhaps I'll fall, be forgotten by all,
All but your mammy and you,
I do my best, along with the rest,
When I march with the brave old boys,
No command is mine, just a number in the line,
For I'm only one of the toys.'

Live entertainment was now restricted to amateur theatrical groups or volunteer organisations. These worked extremely hard during the war, very often under adverse conditions. They not only had to contend with air-raids, the black-out, and electricity cuts but also with shortages of make-up and costumes plus all important props. They struggled on, however, and Norwich owes much to the Police Concert Party which raised funds for blitz victims or dependants of stricken Merchant Navy or Royal Navy ships.

Of course the majority of professional entertainers had by now volunteered for service with ENSA; that body of men and women who brought entertainment to the troops. Many of today's great stars served in ENSA receiving good groundwork for their future careers.

The idea for this unique organisation began one Sunday morning during the summer of 1938 when four great names of the theatre,

Leslie Henson, Basil Dean, Godfrey Tearle and Owen Nares, sat down and discussed plans for bringing live entertainment to the troops. Eventually an official statement was issued to the Press:

'The organisation for the provision of entertainments for His Majesty's Forces both at home and abroad is now completed. The Navy, Army and Air Forces Institutes will be responsible for the organisation, control and finance of the entertainments. The Entertainments National Service Association (ENSA) will provide the entertainments asked for through various committees . . .'

During the early days it was left to Rex Newman, producer of that famous sea-side show *Fol-de-Rols*, to take the first batch of ENSA concert parties to troops stationed in remote corners of the country. With costumes, instruments and odd pieces of hastily built scenery thrown into the back of their lorries which slipped and skidded on ice-bound roads, the artists took their Christmas show on a tour of East Anglian Army camps.

One of Anglia's ENSA volunteers was Norman Lynn of Walton-on-Naze, comedian and ukulele-banjo player. Serving all around Great Britain, the Orkney and Shetland Isles, he later accompanied the advancing Allies into Europe. His stage was anywhere he could

Norman Lynn – one of the many East Anglians who joined ENSA during World War II.

set up his props; even on the back of a lorry or aboard the tossing deck of a ship. He recalls the time when, during one performance in a hospital ward full of wounded servicemen, one of them expired in the middle of his act! It took some doing, trying to be funny in front of chaps who had received such terrible injuries – many fated to spend the rest of their lives in a hospital bed or a wheelchair.

If ENSA was to go down in the history books for its entertainment then the NAAFI must surely be remembered for its culinary achievements. Nearly every service camp sported a NAAFI canteen

where soldiers could purchase the odd comfort or two. Razor blades, pins and needles, blanco, soap and, when stocked, cigarettes and sweets. The canteen girls brought a little feminine warmth to an otherwise drab service outpost. The Norwich NAAFI club, rebuilt on the bombed site of Buntings' in Rampant Horse Street, was considered to be one of the finest canteens in East Anglia, having a dance floor, billiard and table-tennis room as well as a sewing room and luxurious bar.

Bomb damage to Red Lion Street and Rampant Horse Street, Norwich, April 1942. *Photo: G. Swain.*

In this war children were also to play an important part. Apart from the excellent work of Scouts and Guides, Cadets or Observer Corps, younger children were organised into street corps known as 'Cogs'. They served as junior salvage collectors who scavenged from house to house in search of scrap paper and metal. Some idea of their sterling work can be gauged by the 600 tons of scrap metal, paper, textiles, bottles, skins, and even old bones valued at over £2,000 which were collected in Norwich during a twenty-four week period. These youngsters even had an official battle song which started; 'There'll always be a Dustbin!' Working from door to door as the children did very often brought its own reward for a great number of folk gave the junior war-workers their unwanted sweet coupons. This was in fact a great sacrifice, for from a time when a sweetshop's shelves had been crammed with boxes of chocolates and bottles of sweets but now sported nothing but wood or cardboard advertisements, any little extras were always welcome. In fact some old folk spent their spare time cooking home-made toffee, concocted from burnt sugar or black treacle, bicarbonate-of-soda and vinegar, or a slab chocolate made from cocoa powder.

When on 10 July 1940 Lord Beaverbrook issued a national appeal for aluminium scrap it was the 'Cogs' who helped collect and store it in local vacant shops commandeered as salvage centres for the occasion. Through the medium of his newspaper chain Beaverbrook urged everybody to give their all.

'We will turn your pots and pans into Spitfires and Hurricanes, Blenheims and Wellingtons. Everyone who has pots and pans, kettles, vacuum cleaners, hat-pegs, coat-hangers, shoe-trees, bathroom fittings and household ornaments, cigarette boxes or any other articles made wholly or in part of aluminium, should hand them over at once to the local headquarters of the Women's Voluntary Services . . . The need is instant. The call is urgent. Our expectations are high.'

Although on the face of it a very worthwhile scheme, it proved to be yet another Beaverbrook 'bloomer' for much of the scrap was that classed as 'mixed' or 'dirty' metal. Saucepans with iron or tin handles, toys with brass or celluloid extras rivetted or pinned on all had to be removed by hand before they were fit for re-cycling. It was a lengthy process and the necessary man-power just wasn't available to do the job. Much of the scrap was carted away to central depots and left there. At the British Aluminium Company HQ in the Midlands there was, up to a few years ago, a large heap of wartime aluminium scrap kept as a sort of nostalgic memorial.

Part of a Norwich Scout Troop help the war effort by collecting waste paper.

The public responded wonderfully with kettles, colanders, toys, saucepans, jelly moulds, paste-pots and tools cascading upon the centres daily. So much stuff was brought to town and village receiving centres that in some instances it poured out and spilled onto the pavements. Even crashed enemy aircraft were dragged off in the hope of being melted down and re-built to be flown against the original owners.

Aluminium was not the only metal sought after by Whitehall pundits for soon the same madness swept the country again, this time over scrap iron and steel, when a nationwide appeal was made in newspapers and over the air. All around Anglia many fine sets of wrought-iron gates and fences, some dating back to Georgian or Victorian times, fell to the blow-torch of local scrap-dealers. The scars can still be seen on the buildings in the form of jagged iron stumps – silent testimony to a legalised act of vandalism.

Norwich schoolchildren helping the war effort by collecting scrap metal during their holidays.

'Spitfire Fund' was yet another Beaverbrook brainwave which took the country by storm, the idea being that towns and villages around Great Britain and the Commonwealth should raise funds to buy an aircraft. Each town would have their name painted on the side of the 'plane indicating that they had 'paid' for it. The idea didn't end there for by 1943 'Save' weeks were all the in thing. 'War Weapons', 'Wings for Victory', 'Salute the Soldier' and finally 'Thanksgiving Week'. An idea which turned sour on the organisers was that of having a private soldier take the salute at Harwich 'Salute the Soldier Week'. The War Office frowned upon the idea and forbade such action, compromising instead by allowing an NCO to sit beside the high-ranking officers on the saluting base.

Most towns reached their allotted targets and many tanks, ships and aircraft sported Anglian town-names. Men who served aboard these craft were also supplied with comforts raised in the parent town or village.

Village halls pinned up targets setting out a list of items they had pledged to buy. Towns and cities went for something a little larger, usually in the form of a Sunderland flying boat at £50,000 or a corvette at £120,000 . . . another favourite being the Fulman naval fighter at £5,000.

Spitfire	£6,000
Hurricane	£4,500
Blenheim	£17,000
Wellington	£25,000
Pair of binoculars	£17
Hand lead and line	5/-
Chart	6/-
A square yard of deck	£3
Lifebelt or jacket	£3.15.0
Depth Charge	£25
Large life-float	£60
Lewis gun and mounting	£75
Magnetic compass	£150

It was during the Dunkirk crisis that Conscientious Objectors figured prominently in the news. Unlike World War I which had seen a number of nasty incidents when members of various over-zealous, patriotic societies had openly branded C.O.s as cowards or back-sliders, giving any young man out of uniform who walked the street the chance of being accosted and presented with a 'white feather', during the Second World War nobody had seemed to mind very much if you admitted to not wanting to go and fight in a hurry. But once the news of that crushing defeat of British troops on French soil had broken then many stormy letters appeared in local papers accusing the 'conchies' of being 'gutless' and belonging to the 'funk brigade'. County Councillors and other Anglian worthies tried to have these men dismissed from their positions as UDC employees, while even certain Trade Union officials advocated strike action if the 'conchie' was allowed to continue working alongside the men in factories. Some councils, under pressure, did dismiss these men.

Norwich seems to have had the highest number of Conscientious Objectors in the country and the city newspapers carried a great number of articles and correspondence both for and against them.

Many C.O.s did admirable work on the land toiling alongside the Land Army Girls; others joined the Royal Army Medical Corps or went down the mines as 'Bevan Boys'. A number were to play an important part as 'smoke troops', manning smoke-making machines used to screen key towns and cities.

A government leaflet of 1945 advised the female population that, 'Elastic is scarce and still on war service. When your suspenders wear out cut away the worn part and replace with an inch or two of strong tape or braid. Save spare parts . . . never throw away an old corset.' . . . With such adverse effects of clothes shortages it was little wonder that British women felt drab and dowdy as the war ground wearily on. Men, who by and large usually felt more at home in any old pair of trousers, shirt, jumper or jacket, couldn't see what all the fuss was about as the women began to complain bitterly over the cuts and shortages. Those ladies with 'friends' managed to procure service blankets which, once in the hands of an obliging seamstress, could be transformed into a lightweight fashionable coat. There was, of course, a certain edge to be had, however, if a girl did manage to obtain an RAF blanket coat. This was considered far smarter than the Army blanket coat. A higher notch of one-up-manship could be achieved by the woman sporting a re-designed G.I.'s overcoat, for not only was the material superior in quality but her jealous neighbours guessed that she must also be getting other fringe benefits besides!

When the Americans hit East Anglia in 1942 it wasn't only their gigantic war-machine that caused the locals to stop and stare. Once established, they soon took over village and town halls, turning them into miniature American dance halls. To the young, and very often lonely single or newly-wed local girls, the sight and sound of live orchestras, fresh-faced, well-fed G.I.s plus all the excitement of Coca Cola, beer, spirits, ice-cream and cakes caused many to throw moral scruples to the wind. As one wartime typist employed on a Suffolk airbase said: 'Our regular boy friends or husbands were serving away probably doing the same sort of things so why shouldn't we?' 'Live for today – tomorrow may never come!' was their way of reasoning. Dancing was another thing that was dramatically changed almost overnight. No longer did girls stand or sit around the hall like so many wall-flowers waiting for the local lads to pluck up enough courage to ask for a dance. With the American's natural exuberance and high spirits no girl sat around for long. The G.I.s introduced jiving and jitter-bugging . . . a lively form of dancing during which, among the many gymnastic gyrations, the young girl very often found herself tossed upside down or over her partner's shoulder showing her panties to the world. Promiscuity had arrived, or so thought the older generation! US servicemen may not have been very popular with the British males but they certainly stole the hearts of the ladies. During their three year stay in East Anglia they married over 50,000 British girls to be known for all time as 'GI war-brides.'

As the war progressed the first batches of German POWs arrived in East Anglia. Garbed in green or brown-dyed battle dress – with trousers or tunic bearing a large distinctive circle or diamond of contrasting colour – the men worked on farms, airfields or bomb-damaged buildings. Although the British propaganda machine had painted the 'Jerry' as a 'blood-thirsty Hun' reality revealed him to be no different to a British soldier, only wanting an end to the war so he could return to his family.

After work many of the Germans sat in the Nissen huts huddled around a hissing Tilly-lamp, carving from odd pieces of scrap wood splendid examples of treenware. These usually took the form of poker-work peacocks, a family of pecking chickens or tastefully carved platters. Rocking-horses, locomotives and that age-old hobby horse – all were manufactured in the tin huts, arriving at a young customer's bedside with an almost forgotten pre-war shine and gloss of paint. The men had no tools to speak of, only a sharpened table knife or fragment of a cut-throat razor. In a time when everything, even children's toys, was in short supply these German hand-made toys sold as fast as they could be made. Despite the official policy that fraternizing with the enemy was illegal a great number of these pieces found their way into East Anglian homes. Even today, one can very often see these pieces displayed on window-sills or mantle-shelves in cottages around the area. At the time they changed hands for a few cigarettes or a tin of coffee but today they command a high price as a collector's item.

Hand-carved treenware peacock executed by German POW stationed in Essex during World War II.

When not engaged in such lucrative pursuits the men produced impromptu concerts to entertain their fellow prisoners and a few local villagers. Costumes and props were strictly *ersatz* being made from anything they could scrounge; make-up being concocted from lamp-black scraped from Tilly lamp-shades and Cherry Blossom boot polish or dyes.

At Christmas time it was customary to let the Germans attend local church services where their strong foreign dialect competed favourably against those of East Anglian origins.

A group of German POW's shown after a Christmas party in 1945 at Beaumont, Essex. Props and costumes were manufactured from anything that came to hand.

Towards the latter part of the war these men had little or no restraint while in some districts they organised and ran their camps. Once hostilities had ended the prisoners were used to clear land mines from cliff-tops and beaches, after which the mammoth task of repatriation came into being. Many of the men originated from towns and villages now occupied by the Russians and, fearing for their lives or freedom once they had returned, many decided to either stay in Britain or start life afresh in Canada, New Zealand or Australia.

Although one hears very little of enemy prisoners actually escaping from East Anglia during World War II there was one occasion when a party of Luftwaffe POWs tried to steal aircraft from a Suffolk airfield.

Stationed at 186 POW Camp, Colchester, former guard 4808471 Lc/Bm A. Jones, R.A., remembers the night when seven Luftwaffe officers made good their escape from the compound. Once news of the breakout became known a cordon was quickly thrown around the area with roads, houses, and barns being subjected to an exacting search. All attempts to find the missing men failed but eventually news was flashed through that they had at last been recaptured at

Boxstead aerodrome. A post-mortem on the event revealed that, somehow, the group had managed to slip past the patrolling sentries to try and start-up a number of parked fighter 'planes. Failing to work the auxiliary engine which was required to turn over and start the actual aircraft engine, the frustrated party set about sabotaging as many aircraft as possible by pouring into fuel and oil tanks handfuls of sand and gravel. They accounted for quite a few aircraft before they were finally recaptured.

As the war-machine rolled on and with the invasion of Europe on 6 June 1944, people began to scorn air raid warnings and shelters alike. Since the Battle of Britain and the Blitz, air raids had been accepted by the folk of Anglia as just another nuisance like drought or a flood. However, once the V1 or V2 rocket attacks began, people started to use the newly introduced 'Morrison' indoor shelter which had been issued to homes. Experience had shown that this was in fact the only truly effective means of protection. Built along the lines of a large steel box-like zoo cage, the sides were covered with heavy gauge wire mesh. Covered with a table-cloth and used as a sturdy kitchen-table, it was but the work of a moment to lift a corner of the cloth and crawl in to take cover.

One good thing that did come out of the war was the fact that it brought people closer together. Neighbours who perhaps just prior to 1939 had passed only the time of day now helped each other in garden and home. Civilians they may have been, but nearly everyone pulled their weight one way or the other. Women, as we have witnessed, worked absolute wonders and those men not eligible for active service also found little leisure time as service with ARP, CD, AFS, SPC and Observer Corps took all their spare time. From 1 September 1939, CD and ARP members were on a twenty-four-hour-a-day alert. By 1940 the cost of upkeep of ARP in Essex alone was £2,000,000; £375,000 of that sum falling upon the shoulders –or rather the pocket – of the County Council. Air raid shelters for schools were estimated at a further £40,000. The cost overall of the ARP was £30,000,000 a year.

In the Auxiliary Fire Service men trained not only to fight fires but any other hazard that came their way. During the war 793 firemen and twenty-five firewomen were to lose their lives, with over 7,000 being seriously injured. Many suffered from the heat which in a lot of cases caused blindness. Their hours were meant to be a standard forty-eight on and twenty-four off but with heavy fines incurred for absenteeism they worked far in excess of the hours laid down.

Full time AFS men off sick received just three weeks full pay and three weeks half-pay; when injured they received thirteen weeks full pay and were finally dismissed the service if still not fit after that period of time.

May 1941 was to see the formation of a National Fire Service introduced mainly to combat warring factions between town and county brigades. In some instances the chaos that reigned during the early years of the war when a major conflagration was tackled by more than one fire brigade, was vaguely reminiscent of the old insurance company fire brigades when houses were left to burn down because the house bore the wrong fire-mark! Before the war there had been 1,666 local authorities boasting a fire brigade in Britain . . . in the main they could not muster twenty full-time firemen. With the introduction of the NFS with less than fifty 'fire forces' to organise, a far more efficient service was built.

Because, in the early days of the war, water mains could no longer be relied upon to keep up adequate pressure under the stress of a raid, emergency water-tanks each holding 5,000 gallons were situated in most large towns and cities. After a number of fatal accidents involving young children falling into these steel reservoirs it became the practice to cover them over with wire netting.

When the Americans first took up their stations on East Anglian airfields it was the NFS who instructed them in the use of foam fire-fighting equipment and when the invasion was launched, NFS overseas units accompanied the troops across the Channel, doing valuable work on forward fighter bases.

Apart from the fire-fighting, one thing the NFS will surely be remembered best for will be the great number of hand-made toys that the men built during off-watch periods for distribution at children's Christmas parties.

VE-Day[1] was officially announced in East Anglian newspapers on Tuesday 8 May 1945 although in fact the actual ceremony of surrender had taken place on Monday 7 May at 2.41 am (French time). Strange as it may seem, at first folk didn't go as wild as was expected. Newspapers such as the East Essex Gazette brought out special rush editions announcing the good news in banner headlines: 'WAR ENDS IN EUROPE ... GERMANY'S UNCON-DITIONAL SURRENDER'. Alongside the news of Thanksgiving Services and patriotic advertisements such as 'Happier Days are here again' (Tucks Stores), 'Build a New Clacton' (Hodgson & Co., Builders' Merchants) and 'Racing Ahead' (Frank Mitchell 'the

[1]Victory in Europe.

Sportsman's Accountant') one reads the Roll of Honour . . . with over 300 names of local men who had died up to that date. An official announcement gave a foreboding pronouncement that 'There will be few official decorations for VE-Day around the district . . . there being no labour and few decorations.' This may have been official policy but the general public – once the news of hostilities being ended had at last sunk in – started to celebrate wildly. If decorations couldn't be purchased then they made them from paper, sacking, milk-bottle tops and even old newspapers cut into intricate patterns and dyed all the colours of the rainbow. Children's street parties were held with folk pooling their meagre food rations to put on a bumper spread for the excited kids. At night giant bonfires were lit despite official warning that the 'Black-out Tonight 10-18 (Official)' was still in force. Fireworks being non-existent, Home Guard units and locally based sappers set to and came to the rescue using wartime skills to manufacture rockets, bangers and other colourful explosives. Not all proved to be stable for reports of entire bonfires being launched across the village green filtered through from watchful fire brigades. At Walton-on-Naze, effigies of Adolf Hitler, Mussolini, and Hermann Göering sat atop a mountainous bonfire surrounded by a vast crowd of spectators . . . the whole proceedings being completely spoilt when an over-excited former Home Guard threw into the blaze a smoke cannister. On igniting it spouted out thick clouds of bright red smoke; so much so in fact that by the time the audience had finished coughing and choking and the smoke had cleared, bonfire and guys had been consumed by the flames. As if that wasn't bad enough, it was later discovered that everyone who had been standing close to the fire was walking around with bright red faces and hands. White clothing also suffered in a like manner!

Not everybody celebrated the victory with such gusto for a great number of East Anglians had lost members of their family during the six-year struggle. Others had relatives who had been taken prisoner by the Japanese, and it was not known if they were alive or dead. It was to be another three months plus the dropping of the Atomic Bomb before their fate was known.

There were indeed thousands of such men in Japanese hands so starved, ill-treated and disease-ridden that it was a wonder they survived at all, let alone work a full day in factories, paddy-fields or building railways. One such man was Gunner Frank Harwood of Walton-on-Naze, who had joined a light ack-ack Royal Artillery unit at the outbreak of the war. Aged twenty-nine, he found himself posted to the Far East and almost immediately taken prisoner when the Japanese took Singapore.

Harwood must have been blessed with a charmed life for, whilst being transported by ship to Japan, his vessel was torpedoed by the Allies; battened below in the ship's hold together with 386 other Commonwealth prisoners he managed to fight his way to the surface to spend eleven hours in the water before being rescued by the Japanese. Of the original 386 men just forty-three lived to tell the tale.

Once landed on the island of Nagasaki and sufficiently recovered enough to walk, Harwood and the rest of the survivors were put to work in a factory. On 9 August 1945 at approximately 11.40 am Gunner Harwood and a companion were working together near a large concrete trough when the air-raid siren sounded. They listened for the aircraft to pass over and the rush of falling bombs in vain; they heard the aircraft's engines but not the sound of exploding missiles. Making their way back towards their work benches the men winced as a crack like thunder shook the entire building. Throwing himself forward under the concrete trough, Frank suffered only light injuries to his mouth and back. The trough had taken the full weight of falling beams and masonry, thereby saving his life. His comrade, who had tried to make a dash for safety, had suffered the full force of the exploding Atom Bomb.[1]

When Frank Harwood eventually extricated himself from the debris to wander bedraggled and dazed away from the scene of destruction he witnessed many terrible sights. Men, women and young children wandered around the sites of their destroyed homes. Some were completey naked while others had but scorched scraps of clothing hanging together with their shredded, blistered, peeling skin. Disorientated and half-crazed with pain the doomed radio-active victims cried out in vain for water. Making his way towards the coast Gunner Harwood was at last rescued by the advancing Allies. Despite his harrowing ordeal and various tropical diseases he survived to tell his tale and today at a sprightly sixty-seven can still clamber around the steep roof of his terrace house to carry out repairs. The radio-active death which was to claim thousands of innocent Japanese victims had passed him by.

Other returning POWs were not as lucky as Frank Harwood, for the ravages of confinement and privation had badly afflicted many both in mind and body leaving them unfit for future gainful employment. At the beginning of the war the armed forces numbered

[1]The A-Bomb measured 10 ft 8 in long by 5 ft diameter. It was nick-named 'Fat Man' after Winston Churchill.

only 381,000 but by the end over 5,900,000 had served King and Country. 265,000 were killed, 277,000 received wounds and 172,000 were taken prisoner.

CHAPTER FIVE

GOTT STRAFE EAST ENGLAND

During the First World War East Anglia had witnessed a number of Zeppelin and Gotha bomber raids, and in fact if one studies the flight charts of the Imperial German Air Force one can see that the air-space over our part of the country was fairly thickly woven with a mass of criss-cross lines and patterns as the flights of bombers passed back and forth.

Of course in 1939 the civilian population had very little idea of what to expect once the bombs began to fall. Older folk who had experienced World War I bombing raids tried to convey some sort of word picture, even bringing out the old yellowing and faded photographs which showed, in a limited way, the sort of damage one could expect. Enemy missiles dropped over Britain during World War I by the Gotha bombers usually consisted of five 50kg or a couple of 100kg bombs but on a long journey it was common practice not to exceed a bomb load of 500kg. However, by January 1918 (just ten months before the armistice) a giant 1,000kg (2,200lb) PuW bomb was being carried slung beneath the fuselage of a Friedrichshafen GIIIa. Some 710 of these giant bombs fell on Allied targets.

No, there was just no way of knowing what to expect. In World War I the number of civilians killed in enemy air raids on the UK was 1,413. In World War II it was to be 60,595, victims of some 70,995 tons of H.E. which destroyed 220,000 homes and damaged nearly five million more.

Early in World War II the Luftwaffe took to dropping sea-mines by parachute. Measuring 8ft x 2ft in diameter, the British dubbed these lethal cylinders 'landmines'. A tremendous amount of damage was inflicted on factories and houses by this mine. Another favourite bomb used by the Luftwaffe was the thermite incendiary which weighed about 2lb and measured some eighteen inches long. These were dropped in a special container nick-named 'Hermann's bread-basket' holding about seventy-three bombs. Later a new type of incendiary bomb container was introduced, capable of holding 1,000 I.Bs. Originally it was common practice for wardens and house-holders to tackle these bombs by smothering them with a dustbin lid or a shovelful of earth or sand. Something of a national sport was evolved around these magnesium bombs for we read stirring accounts of frail old ladies and gentlemen hopping around the streets and gardens cornering and dousing large numbers of flaring bombs. On the face of it, all good patriotic fun; for if the bomb was caught in the early stages before taking hold of a road surface or other inflammable material little harm was done. However, later more improved versions were fitted with an explosive charge and near Felixstowe we hear of a farm labourer killed whilst trying to pull an unexploded 1kg incendiary bomb out of a field.

In the later stages of the war a great number of people – including young children – were injured by tampering with incendiary bombs and unexploded bullets.

The 'phoney' war came abruptly to a halt in the British Isles when twenty-seven year old James Isbister from the Bridge of Waith, Orkney, fell in a strafing raid in April 1940. In England the first civilian casualties to die through enemy action were at the popular seaside resort of Clacton-on-Sea. Actually the whole incident was the outcome of a terrible accident. Just before the witching hour of midnight on the night of 30 April 1940 a Heinkel IIIE bomber of the 3rd Squadron Combat Wing 126 had been engaged on a mine-laying mission off the Suffolk/Norfolk coast. Diving into a dense blanket of sea-fog it flew around until it broke clear just above Harwich. Here it was spotted by the AA guns who opened fire at once, one shell exploding close to the tail causing extensive damage to the rudder. Flying in ever decreasing circles the 'plane found itself over the town of Clacton. Here the story is taken up by a member of the local fire brigade . . .

'At the station we heard the sound of this low-flying aircraft and by the strange noises she was making we reckoned something was drastically wrong with her. She came overhead, circled the town twice, went out to sea then turned towards Holland-on-Sea and came down low over the recreation ground as though trying to land.'

If the pilot had indeed been trying to land his stricken aircraft on that plot of open ground then something went dramatically wrong with his controls for the 'plane overshot the field, knocking two or three chimney pots off on the way, bounced over a lamp standard, then finished up against the side of a house.

Eye-witness accounts stress that flames had been seen flickering around the fuselage as the aircraft had tried to make a forced landing.

Once the sound of screaming, tortured metal had subsided a strange stillness seemed to hang over the smouldering wreckage as black smoke and brick dust rose in lazy unison. Some folk thought it was only a few seconds, while others swear it was some minutes before the whole area was devastated by an ear-bursting, earth-shaking explosion. People who had been running towards the scene of the crash were picked up bodily and thrown around the streets like so many leaves in an autumn gale. Others, standing close to windows and peering out into the darkness, had faces and bodies slashed to shreds by flying glass. One man, 150 yards from the explosion, felt something strike him across the chest. Grabbing the warm, sticky object with both hands, he found to his dismay that he was clutching a shattered dismembered limb!

Although fire, ambulance, ARP and police organisations had been practising continuously for such an event, the forces attending the blasted area surprised even the authorities. The way they handled the crisis and the speed with which the wounded were taken to safety established something of a criterion among rescue teams of other future bombed towns.

Extensive damage caused by the Heinkel IIIE which crashed in Victoria Road, Clacton-on-Sea, causing the first civilian casualties of the war.

Many of the 160 injured need never have suffered if only they had heeded the warnings of the authorities. It was discovered, during the de-briefing, that many of the injuries had been sustained by flying glass and debris caused by people standing at closed windows and doorways or even running to view the crash. If they had only taken to their garden shelters when the warning was first given, casualties would certainly have been much lighter.

Roads and avenues around the devastated block were littered with debris. Tall trees, split and scorched by the full force of the explosion, swayed drunkenly in the light, early morning breeze. Bushes and garden shrubs, only yesterday garbed in their spring finery, stood naked and exposed, their shocked twigs protesting to the open skies.

Our fireman continues his narrative:

'We were on our way to where we thought the aircraft must have landed when we felt and heard the explosion. When we eventually arrived a few minutes later it was a terrible sight which greeted us. The spot where Mr and Mrs Gill's house had stood was completely flattened with only a great pile of bricks and rubble left. What was left of the 'plane had been tossed against the wall of a nearby house, the wings torn off and lying to one side. About twenty yards away we found the bodies of the four German airmen all black and burned.'

The wreckage of the Heinkel IIIE, and the scorched trees close by.

Another part of the wreckage of the Heinkel IIIE, showing the damage caused to an adjacent house, with windows shattered and roof-tiles stripped.

The news of the air-crash certainly made headlines, for although classed as a restricted area the world's press really went to town. Reporters and cameramen flocked into the town to interview survivors and members of the rescue teams. Ironically, local newspapers respected the restrictions imposed by the authorities and refrained from publishing any photographs of the damage. Instead, when they at last thought of so doing they had to borrow them from the national newspapers. It so happened that one of these photographs found its way into a German orientated newspaper, becoming the talking point of German nationals the world over.

Local councillors protested vigorously in an attempt to have the story suppressed but to little avail . . . Clacton-on-Sea was big war news and the appetite of a war-news-starved public had to be satiated. If the businessmen of the town had reckoned that suppressing the news would have saved their forthcoming season they needn't have bothered for the Government cancelled the Whitsun altogether, finally bringing home to one and all that holidays were a thing of the past for the next few years.

Leutnant und Beobackter Hermann Sodtmann, aged 24, one of the crew of the ill-fated Heinkel IIIE.

Once the news had been published via wireless and press media, people with relatives living in or near Clacton flooded the GPO with over 3,106 panic calls . . . the average number of telegrams handled daily in 1939 was 275! Instead of the usual five messenger boys, GPO authorities had to call upon the services of an extra fourteen postmen using cycles, vans and motorcycles.

It was decided that the four German airmen should be buried with full military honours at the local cemetery on 4 May. Crowds lined the route as RAF lorries carrying the swastika-draped coffins drove through the town and out towards the graveyard at Burrsville. Other than the slow tread of marching feet as airmen and members of local organisations passed by, one could hear the sobbing of many of the womenfolk. As one policeman recalls: 'It was obvious what these women were thinking: "There but for the grace of God go my sons." '

Extra police reinforcements had indeed been drafted into the district as a precaution against any hostile demonstrations. Despite a general outcry from certain quarters of the more popular press, the gallant foe were laid to rest amidst numerous floral tributes, their coffins being covered with wreaths of lilies, irises and other spring

Burial of the four German airmen who lost their lives when their Heinkel IIIE bomber crashed on Clacton on the night of 30 April/1 May 1940. They belonged to the 3rd Squadron Combat Wing 126 (Heinkel Bombers).

flowers. Inscriptions ranged from: 'From all ranks of the Royal Air Force', 'With deepest sympathy, from RAF Martlesham Heath', to 'With heartfelt sympathy from a Mother'. Children threw bunches of wallflowers and primroses onto the coffins as they were slowly lowered to their temporary resting place[1] accompanied by a volley of shots from the honour party.

The names of those Luftwaffe men who had helped make war history over East Anglia were:

Oberleutnant und Flugzeugführer
Hermann VAGTS. Age 25

Leutnant und Beobackter
Hermann SODTMANN. Age 24

Unteroffizier und Bordmechaniker
Karl-Heinz FRESEN. Age 26

Unteroffizier und Bordfunker
Hans-Günther KOCH. Age 21

For some days after the crash the area swarmed with staff officers and Air Ministry technicians searching the wreckage to try and glean something about Luftwaffe technology. They had reckoned without the homing instincts of the souvenir hunters who had been quick off the mark . . . tools, instruments, the compass, bits of the engine and even part of the tail-plane had been spirited away.[2] My fireman friend who had been searching the inside of the shattered fuselage had stumbled across a leather Luftwaffe belt; brand-new and with hardly a sign of wear, it bore on the inside printed with indelible pencil the name 'Fresen'.

An amusing incident which is still joked about among older folk in the town is the unique discovery of the 'bomb'.

Ex-fireman Reg Lawes recounts the oft-told tale with a wry grin: 'It was the following morning while we were taking a well-earned break from clearing up some of the wreckage that this fellow came over to us lads. About half-a-dozen of us were having a smoke and a rest, sitting on what we took to be a giant galvanised water tank. He asked us if we'd mind shifting off a while as he wanted to examine our perch a little more closely. Examine it he did for he and another Royal Navy bloke started to unscrew bits and bobs off the side of the thing. Imagine our dismay and excitement when they told us what our water tank really was . . . an unexploded landmine! We never did live that one down.'

[1]German war dead were exhumed in 1968 and re-interred at Cannock Chase, Staffordshire.

[2]When first I started gathering information for this book a woman brought me a Luftwaffe knife. It seems that her husband had found it the morning after the crash, tucked away in a concealed pocket of a flying-boot which had been buried in a pile of loose rubble.

War had come to East Anglia and the following week newspapers carried a block advertisement published by the John Bull Magazine offering free insurance to all its readers . . . 'John Bull's £200 Air Raid Policy' it was called. Alongside appeared another sober advertisement for air-raid shelters.

RE-INFORCED CONCRETE SHELTERS
FOR DOMESTIC PURPOSES

Designed to Home Office Requirements. The shelter gives full protection against the greater danger of falling debris, splinters and blast caused by high explosive bombs falling nearby; the chances of a direct hit being very small.

It is permanent and substantial, will not rust or deteriorate, and is quickly erected by unskilled labour. In normal times it can be used as a coal cellar, fruit and vegetable store, or tool shed. Owing to the unit construction of this shelter the length can be increased at a reasonable charge to accommodate more people.

The domestic type to accommodate four persons delivered to your site price £13.10.0d. Prices for larger accommodation on application.

This shelter also solves the problem for Schools, Works, Institutions, etc, and designs will be sent on application suitable to accommodate 12, 24 or 48 persons.

In spite of the advertisement being displayed alongside the full report of the extensive damage, the firm in question only sold one shelter!

Now the pace began to warm up. The time for honouring fallen Luftwaffe crews with full military funerals had slipped away. As the enemy began to carry out more raids the ordinary folk started to play an important part. Identification of aircraft became a national pastime and almost a sport – even school children could pick out the finer points of tail units, cockpit assembly and wingtips. Time after time you would hear someone shout out as a flight of aircraft hove into view: 'Take cover – Jerry's coming!' Then above the ensuing rush and tumble, a knowing voice would pipe up: 'Don't flap – it's one of ours. I'd know those wings anywhere!'

The skies seemed never empty of aircraft, both allied as well as the ever-increasing enemy. Although in the early days Britain's war machine was rather weak and thin upon the ground, during the spring of 1940 production of aircraft was noticeably increased. The early model Spitfire had a tank capable of taking eighty gallons of fuel but later this was to be increased to 210 gallons. The pride of the Luftwaffe was the single-seater Me 109 which proved to be the equal – at 370 mph – to the Spitfire. It was superior to the Hurricane, also

The C-type mine after being de-
fused by Lt. Cdr. R.J.H. Ryan
and Chief Petty Officer R.V.
Ellingworth. Before being de-
activated, the mine served as a
seat for many men. They
thought it was an old hot-water
cylinder. Both of these naval
men were to be awarded the
George Cross, but lost their
lives examining an unexploded
mine at Dagenham, Essex.

CLACTON
NAZI RAIDER CRASH!

Every Family is urged to take immediate
advantage of

"JOHN BULL'S"
£200 AIR RAID
INSURANCE
(Underwritten at LLOYDS)

FREE!
FOR EVERY READER
JOHN BULL
EVERY THURSDAY - 2d.

★ *Fill in the Newsagent's Order Form on right now and hand it to your newsagent as soon as possible. Fill in the Registration Form also and post it at once to "John Bull."*

─── SIGN TO-DAY ───

JOHN BULL
Hand this Form to Your Newsagent.

To (Name of Newsagent) ....

Address ....

Please deliver or reserve JOHN BULL for me weekly until further notice.

Signature ....

Address ....

Date ....

PLEASE WRITE CLEARLY.
C.G. 3.5.1940

POST THIS FORM TO
John Bull," Registration Department, 128, Long Acre. London W C 2.

I have sent an Order Form to my Newsagent for the regular weekly delivery of JOHN BULL. Please register me as a regular reader.

Reader's Signature

Age ....

Address ....

Name and Address of Newsagent

Use 1d. stamp. Don't seal envelope. A Certificate setting out the full Benefits and Conditions and certifying registration will be sent if 1d. stamped addressed envelope is enclosed for return.

PLEASE WRITE CLEARLY. C.G. 3.5.1940

having eight machine guns, but its one great fault revolved around its flying time. As it could only carry enough fuel to stay airborne for 1½ hours its actual fighting time over Britain was but a few minutes. Of its stable mates, the Me 110 was far too unwieldy and the much-exalted Stuka slow and poorly armed.

On 13 June 1940 it was the harbour of Harwich which shook to the sound of an exploding aircraft. A Hampden bomber of 144 Squadron stationed at Helmswell, Lincolnshire, dropped a series of red and green recognition flares over the blacked-out harbour. Obviously in serious trouble it fouled the cable of a barrage balloon and crashed into Marriage's Flour Mill, setting fire to the mill, four barges which were tied up alongside (these being Golden Grain, Phoenician, The Millar and Rayjohn) plus five railway trucks. The five crew members all perished in the ensuing conflagration and a Mr D. Grayling, who had worked nearby, died of his injuries.

Norwich, that most important Norfolk city and the very heart of East Anglia, was to suffer its first baptism of enemy fire on the warm summer afternoon of 9 July. No air-raid had been sounded when from the north-east two low-flying aircraft screamed in over the city. The first thing that the unaware populace knew of the attack was the harsh crackle of machine-gun fire and whistle of falling bombs. Boulton and Paul, famous for engineering and now manufacturing parts for Horsa gliders and Oxford Trainer aircraft, received the full fury of the bombing with ten of their workers losing their lives and many more injured. The nearby locomotive sheds of the London and North Eastern Railways were also extensively damaged. One eye-witness thought that the heap of bent, twisted and almost sculptured railway lines reminded him of giant sticks of twisted liquorice! In that raid twenty-seven townsfolk died and a great number were maimed and injured.

It was after the evacuation of Dunkirk that the Battle of Britain really began to swing into full fury. Invasion fever was in the air again and plans were hurriedly introduced to foil the landing of gliders and aircraft on golf courses, fields and recreation grounds. Around the east coast open fields could be seen bristling with rows of stout poles bearing lengths of wire strung across the tops.

Left: 'John Bull's' £200 air raid insurance.

Golf clubs with plenty of open space proved very popular for both allied and enemy aircraft when making emergency or crash landings. Consequently golfers' rules had to be amended and temporary provisions for dealing with such nuisances entered in the Golfer's Handbook.

(i) Players are asked to collect bomb and shell splinters to save these causing damage to the mowing machines.

(ii) In competition, during gunfire or while bombs are falling, players may take cover without penalty for ceasing play.

(iii) The positions of known delayed-action bombs are marked by red and white flags placed at reasonably, but not guaranteed, safe distances.

(iv) A ball lying in a crater may be lifted and dropped not nearer the hole without penalty.

(v) A ball moved by enemy action may be replaced as near as possible to where it lay, or if lost or destroyed a ball may be dropped not nearer the hole without penalty.

(vi) A player whose stroke is affected by the simultaneous explosion of a bomb or shell, or machine-gun fire, may play another ball from the same place. Penalty, one stroke.

During the war 'plane crashes were all part of everyday life. When one considers that a total of 677 RAF aircraft crashed in Norfolk alone between the outbreak of hostilities and 31 May 1945, which included no fewer than ninety-two Wellington bombers, one can get a fair idea of the numbers that fell on the rest of East Anglia.

Reading through a police incident report on war crashes gives one a little insight of the situation.

31/8/40   Hawker Hurricane I P 3383 Fg.O. M.G. Doulton, 601 Sq Debden Cat.3. Missing. Shot down by Messerschmitts and crashed into the River Colne off Aldboro' Point. Pilot killed previous to crash, 'plane buried in mud and non-recoverable.

31/8/40   Junkers Ju 88 shot down and crashed into mud flat off East Mersea gun position near Mersea Stone. Plane wrecked.

31/8/40   Unidentified aircraft (believed Ju 88) shot down and crashed into water in mouth of River Colne. Plane lost, fate of crew not known.

31/8/40   Heinkel He III shot down and destroyed by fire at point 880yds S.E. of Hill Farm, Layer, near Abbeton. III KG 53 Legion Condor Lille-Nord Codes AI – Oblt Huhn, Gefr Erwin Gleissner and two others unknown killed, one taken POW. Time 1604 hrs.

31/8/40	Messerschmitt Bf 110 shot down and destroyed at Flories Farm, Great Tey. Plane exploded, crew killed. Time 1625 hrs.
2/10/40	Junkers Ju 88 shot down during the night and crashed to the rear of the sewage works at Brightlingsea. Plane partially damaged, crew captured. 0200 hrs.
29/10/40	Messerschmitt Bf 109 shot down and crashed at Langenhoe Lodge near Langenhoe, pilot captured unhurt. 1600 hrs (approx).

In wartime, facts do have a tendency to become a little distorted especially if a lot of activity is reported around one particular area. Such was the case of the lost Me 110 which was shot down during a dog-fight one evening in mid-August.

To be fully acquainted with the entire story one will have to swing back the clock to the summer's day of 18 August 1940. All day from early morning the might of the German Luftwaffe had roared in over the English Channel to pick out numerous choice targets. All day the Battle of Britain few had skimmed across the East Anglian country-side to intercept and do battle with a determined enemy. Losses had been high on both sides and around mid-afternoon a lull had taken place almost as though the Germans were respecting English tea-time!

It was just after tea in fact, at approximately 1645 hrs that a flight of enemy aircraft were observed approaching from the east, their engines throbbing with that all-too familiar rhythm. In all, there were over one hundred enemy aircraft in that flight.

Mr H. Page of Great Clacton, home on leave from the service at the time, recalls the scene all too well:

'I remember my old mother called me out into the garden to see what she thought was a swarm a bees hovering above our apple tree. Instead of bees I saw nearly a hundred German 'planes flying that high that they had white exhaust trails standing out against the clear blue sky. Next thing I saw was about six or maybe seven British fighters – no more that's for sure – come skimming over the rooftops and right up among them Jerries. They scattered all over the place with one lot of bombers making towards the south. The others stayed to fight and the whole sky was taken up with diving, wheeling, fighting aircraft.'

One of these, a Messerschmitt Bf 110, was seen to be hit and came diving down with thick black smoke pouring from its burning engines closely followed by a lone British fighter. With engines screaming at full throttle this 39ft long, twin-engined fighter dived into the centre of the town.

An on-the-spot eye-witness was Patrol Officer Frederick Wolton serving with the local brigade. His was the first Fire Tender to arrive at the scene and he recalls: 'I shall always remember that dreadful scream of engines as the Me 110 dived towards earth, at the time I would have sworn right towards us. After the soft, dull sound of the crash our one thought was for the poor devils that must surely be trapped in the smitten houses in that area. It came as something of a shock when we did at last find the spot . . . nothing at all damaged, not even a pane of glass was broken. Of the enemy aircraft there was nothing either, only a hole in the ground and the heap of wet sand slowly sliding back into the mucky water of the pond. The only evidence of anything untoward was a few small fires among the surrounding wild bushes and a few pieces of shattered aluminium . . . just enough to fill a small wheelbarrow.'

Police and RAF authorities visited the spot and even put steel rods down in the pond to a depth of nineteen feet but feeling nothing of the aircraft left it in the bowels of the sandpit.

The crew who tackled the bush fires after an Me 110 crashed into Smith's Sandpits.

Group Captain Colin F. Gray, the New Zealand Air Force pilot who shot down the Me 110 which took its crew of two down into the depths of Smith's Pit on 18 August 1940. They are still there!

This same scene was being enacted all over the British Isles during this stage of the offensive. Dozens of aircraft crash-dived into fields, rivers, even ponds and backwaters; in fact along the East Anglian coastline there are still a number of wrecks which cause untold havoc and damage to the equipment of inshore fisherfolk.

We read so much of the Battle of Britain with many flippant references to the whole thing being nothing more than an 'exciting game of cricket' that it makes refreshing reading to hear what a former Battle of Britain pilot thought of the action. Group Captain Colin Gray, DFC, DSO, late of the New Zealand Air Force and serving in Anglia with RAF 54 Squadron during World War II writes: 'It was no picnic despite what anyone might say later . . . most of us were pretty scared all the bloody time.' The pilot who had been responsible for shooting down the aforementioned Me 110 was in fact this same

Colin Gray, then just another pilot officer, fighting in the Battle of Britain. Of the Me 110's destruction he recalls:

'This aircraft pulled up vertically in front of me as I fired and I have always assumed that the pilot and rear gunner must have been killed because it appeared to do a wing over and dive straight down into the middle of Clacton-on-Sea. The Me 110 was travelling very fast in the dive and although I attempted to follow initially, I soon gave this up as a bad job and watched it spiral down all the way until it crashed. I certainly did not see anyone bail out.'

In RAF records we find a short, cryptic message – so many enemy aircraft had been destroyed over British shores that day that both British and German records are somewhat brief.

'Clacton (Smith Sandpits) (Me 110) on 18/8/40. A/C hit ground hard – smashed completely. No identification of any kind possible. A/C type from local reports.'

Luftwaffe records for that day list only three missing aircraft that fit this Me 110's description, time and location, all coming from the ZG 26 Stab. On the actual face of the matter one would think that this is the end of the whole affair but one important clue has come to light over the years. A former Special Constable, upon hearing of the current interest in this lost aircraft, dug out of his china cabinet a small hand-made model of a Me 110. Mounted on a metal base bearing a metal name-tag the model had been beaten and forged out of scrap aluminium . . . the tag bore the following legend:

| Mtt | A.G. | 3526 | 17 |
| 110 | 14 | 04 (285) | 96 |

Special Constable W.A. Rampling had been ordered to keep idle onlookers away from the scene of the crash and whilst so doing chanced to stumble across a small piece of battered aluminium bearing the name tag. Slipping it into his pocket he took it home to make the model of this crashed German aircraft, a memento of his particular war.

Contact was established with the Luftwaffe authorities regarding the specifications on the name-tag, but unfortunately as a great number of their records were destroyed during Allied bombing raids, little is hoped to be gained from that source. Who knows, perhaps one day in the not too distant future an old Luftwaffe Battle of Britain pilot will read this account and remember the day when two of his former comrades plunged to their death over Clacton[1].

[1]Since going to press, further research has finally established that the two men, Hauptmann Hubert Leuttke and Unteroffizier Herbert Brillo, did in fact belong to the 4th Staffel of ZG 26.

Today, Smith Sandpits as such no longer exist, for during the 1950s and '60s the entire area was filled in with household refuse and builders' rubble, finally to be levelled off and made into an industrial estate. It is now called Ford Road. The wreckage of the 'plane still remains deep in the sand while the two crewmen sleep the long sleep of the dead in their own rather unique Valhalla.

Over Chelmsford a rear gunner from a crippled Heinkel managed to jump to safety with his parachute only partially opened. Landing in a field near the village of Althorne he managed, although badly injured, to stagger to a nearby cottage and knock at the door. It was answered by Mrs Margaret Windridge, who was rather taken aback by the sight of the blood-stained figure framed in the doorway weakly waving a pistol about. He meant no harm however, only wishing to surrender his firearm. Dressing his wounds and treating him for shock Mrs Windridge cared for him until a local military escort arrived to take him prisoner. She still retains his service first aid kit and when from time to time she finds it often wonders what ever became of that young airman, for she never did learn his identity.

Not all crashed airmen were that lucky, as for ordinary folk one airman looked very much the same as another despite the authorities issuing posters and notices to the effect that British pilots had two parachutes; one a small pilot chute followed by the larger main one.

One particular British fighter pilot whose 'plane had been shot down in flames over East Anglia found himself drifting by parachute down towards a fruit farm. Becoming ensnared in one of the trees he swayed back and forth, far too badly burned about face and hands to free himself. Barely half conscious he observed through his swollen eyelids a group of people running towards him. It was the farmer, his wife and young son. Only just managing to croak out a few unintelligible words – his lips also distorted with burns – he tried in vain to tell them that he was British. He needn't have bothered, for the farmer, thinking he had a Hun up his tree, kept jabbing the helpless flyer with his wicked-looking pitchfork. All the while the farmer's son was running around the tree threatening the airman in language quite unfit for a small boy; this performance being eventually brought to a halt with the brat having his ears soundly boxed by his irate mother. As the injured airman painfully swooned away again he remembers the woman taking the lad to task for using foul language on a Sunday!

With ever-increasing air activity many strange and sometimes peculiar incidents took place involving both airmen and aircraft. During the early hours on the morning of 5 July 1941 a light trainer aircraft flew in over the Essex coast and landed in a field close to the village of Thorpe-le-Soken. On the face of it this was nothing very unusual for at this period in time country folk had become used to seeing the odd 'plane or two touching down in a handy field. Lack of fuel, faulty instruments or even badly shot-up aircraft were often dropping in, so to speak. However, this aircraft was no casual caller. The crew of two had just made a daring and adventurous escape from enemy-occupied Belgium. They were two sergeant pilots of the Belgian Air Force, Michel Donnet and Leon Divoy.

Theirs is an interesting tale to tell, one of intrigue, spirit and a schoolboy sense of adventure.

Having participated in the short-lived campaign of 1940, Sergeant Michel Donnet was taken prisoner soon after the humiliating Belgian capitulation, spending seven months kicking his heels in a German POW camp. Repatriation came in 1941 and he soon found himself trying to think up various ways of escaping to Britain. All of these seemed doomed to failure until it was brought to his notice that an old SV4B light trainer aircraft was still standing unguarded in a shed just a few miles from his home. Contacting a fellow pilot, Leon Divoy, they worked under cover of darkness on the disabled 'plane. Instruments which were almost non-existent or damaged had to be

One that got away! The SV4B trainer in which Sergeant Pilot Michel Donnet and Leon Divoy made good their escape from German-occupied Belgium in 1941. This photo, taken at an RAF station, shows the 'plane with its newly-painted RAF insignia and camouflage. Seated is Michel Donnet.

repaired or prefabricated from odds and ends including parts from an old alarm clock. Fuel was to prove something of a major problem, but with the help of Sgt Divoy he managed to refine enough from ordinary petrol purchased on the black-market (being run, as it turned out, by a German serviceman!). By 4 July 1941 all was ready so, donning their Belgian uniforms and roughly painting Belgian roundels on the wings of their 'liberated' aircraft, they took off on a journey into the unknown.

Because of the chronic shortage of fuel the two men had been unable to test the engine beforehand. Even so, if extra had been available it would have been far too dangerous to start-up the noisy engine as there were German patrols deployed in the district.

Luck proved to be on their side for after a fair bit of coughing and spluttering the engine started with a roar and off they flew over the startled heads of a nearby German patrol. Although harassed by enemy flak and searchlights all the way to the coast they ran the gauntlet without any serious damage to themselves or the 'plane.

Out over the North Sea their engine started to fail and they were forced to descend to 1,000 feet. Diving through a cloud bank, Donnet discovered that at long last they were over land but his next glance sent his heart down to his boots. There, down through the wispy clouds, he observed the roof of what appeared to him to be an aircraft hanger, bearing in bold letters the legend 'HOLLAND'. He couldn't believe it! After all they had been through it had been all in vain to fly round in a giant circle and land in enemy-held Holland. With only enough fuel left in the tank for another twenty minutes of actual flying he coasted down in search of a suitable landing-strip. Making a successful touch-down (as it so happened near Daken's Farm, Frinton Road, Thorpe-le-Soken), Donnet and Divoy pushed the aircraft under a clump of trees at the same time hiding their charts, documents and firearms in the nearby bushes, for as Donnet says: 'We actually thought that after seeing HOLLAND on that rooftop we were in fact in that country.'

If only they had seen the other side of that roof they would have seen the rest of the message . . .'MOTORS' . . . a garage known as Holland Motors of Holland-on-Sea, Essex.[1]

Somewhat crestfallen, the two airmen wandered along the pleasant country lanes hoping that eventually someone, somewhere would appear to take them into protective custody. Strange things could befall wandering servicemen in enemy-held territory!

[1]Whereas the British had been most thorough in removing street and road signs they had, in a lot of cases, forgotten such things as the business addresses cast into manhole covers and drain grills. In this instance the name on the garage roof had been overlooked.

Out on patrol, Sergeant Percy Brown of the local constabulary had in fact seen and heard the light aircraft dip down behind the clump of trees, and was making his way towards that spot when he stumbled across the two men walking towards him and making obvious signs that they wished to surrender.

Once back at the Thorpe police station the two men managed to convey to Sergeant Brown just where they had come from and who they were. As documentary evidence of their identity had been left near their 'plane it was decided to send Divoy, escorted by Special Constable Charles Childs, back to the scene of the landing to recover the vital documents and search the Stampe trainer. By now the two airmen had realised that they were in fact in Great Britain and not Holland . . .

Eventually Donnet and Divoy were taken to London and after a suitable period of interrogation joined the RAF.

Michel Donnet was posted as a pilot officer with 64 fighter squadron together with his friend Divoy. Donnet was to end the war as a Colonel with 375 combat missions to his credit, three enemy aircraft destroyed and damage to six others. He holds the D.F.C. and Belgian Croix de Guerre together with four citations.

Leon Divoy spent the rest of his war in a German POW camp, for one day in April 1942, whilst on patrol over occupied France, he collided with another Spitfire and crash-landed.

Some years ago Colonel Donnet paid a visit to the scene of his wartime adventures in the hope of holding a reunion with his wartime 'captors' but alas, time had taken its toll for Sergeant Brown had died the previous year, leaving seventy-eight-year-old Charles Childs the sole surviving witness to the strange exciting saga.

At the end of the war the old Stampe Vertongen 4B Reg. No. 00-ATD was ferried back to Belgium where today it can be seen on display in the Musée de l'Armée in Brussels.

By early spring of 1942 plans were being formulated by Sir Arthur 'Bomber' Harris, Commander-in-Chief of Bomber Command, together with Frederick Lindemann, the Prime Minister's Scientific Adviser, to carry out indiscriminate firebomb attacks on the working class houses in Germany, in addition to the frequent heavy raids on the industrial district of the Ruhr. Experimental raids started on the nights of 28-29 March against the picturesque port of Lubeck, an historic town of impressive beauty. As Harris records[1]: 'It was not a vital target but it seemed to me better to destroy an industrial town of moderate importance than to fail to destroy a large industrial city.'

[1]*Bomber Offensive*. Sir Arthur Harris.

A selection of propaganda books sold by His Majesty's Stationery Office as morale boosters.

In the ensuing raid half of Lubeck was destroyed by a concentrated incendiary attack. Hitler retaliated at once, giving birth to the so-called Baedeker raids[1]. In these raids the Germans deliberately picked out targets which boasted extremely fine examples of Tudor or Georgian architecture and with poor defences. On the night of 27/28 and 29/30 April Norwich was the chosen victim. On the Monday night the sirens sounded at 23.21 hours heralding a raid which was to last for two hours during which time 185 H.E. bombs weighing 50 tons were dropped. 162 people died in that reprisal raid with over 600 injured. Come Wednesday and another night of terror with a raid which lasted for an hour-and-a-quarter. Sixty-nine people died and eighty-nine were injured under the onslaught of 112 high-explosive bombs and machine gun fire[2]. Add to this the effect of falling shrapnel from low-firing AA guns and one has some idea of the hardship endured by the stoic Norwich citizens. Reprisal raids had come to stay . . . and Harris went on to bigger and better raids starting with the first 1,000 bomber raid on Cologne on 30 May.

Assembling every able-bodied man and 'plane he could find – which included inexperienced crews and obsolete aircraft – he

[1]Hitler used a copy of Baedeker's *British Isles*; a pre-war guide book to places of historic interest.

[2]*Norwich at War*, Joan Banger.

Above: Bomb damage in St Stephen's Street, Norwich, April 1942. *Photo: G. Swain.*

Below: A Dornier 17 German bomber which was shot down over Norfolk, and exhibited in Eaton Park, Norwich, in the early 1940s.

launched the RAF's first 1,000 bomber raid against the city of Cologne. Later reports revealed that over six hundred acres of the city had been completely destroyed with the subsequent firestorm incinerating literally thousands of the civilian population.

One of the luckiest men alive who took part in the Cologne raid must surely be number 638234 Sergeant Flight Engineer Harold W. Curtis who flew with 78 Squadron.

Returning from the raid, Sergeant Curtis's Halifax Mark I bomber was involved in a mid-air collision with a Hampden bomber over March, Cambridge. With both aircraft tumbling to the ground in a mass of flames Curtis managed to throw himself from the doomed aircraft, his parachute only just opening at 200 feet. Landing heavily he badly wrenched his left leg but still managed to hobble over to the wreckage and assist local Home Guard to remove the dead and injured. A humorous side to this story (although as Sergeant Curtis points out, not to him at the actual time!) was due to the action of an over-zealous Home Guard who, spotting a parachute flare among the debris, promptly evacuated the entire area, leaving the lame sergeant stranded in the middle of the field. The poor fellow had to limp back towards the main road almost a mile-and-a-half before being picked up by a local doctor driving an ancient Austin motorcar.

638234 Sgt. Flight Engineer Harold W. Curtis of 78 Squadron. A crew-member of a 'Halifax' Mark I bomber returning from the first 1,000 bomber raid on Cologne on 30 May 1942, he was involved in a mid-air collision over March, Cambridge . . . and lived to tell the tale!

Bombing raids still continued around East Anglia but the population had, by now, grown used to the sound of falling bombs and unless it was a bit too near for comfort carried on at work or play as though nothing untoward was happening. Norwich was receiving more than its fair share of attention and over 139 public houses were destroyed or damaged in raids during 1942.

By now the Americans had entered the conflict and East Anglia was to play host to our US cousins for the duration of the war. Norwich, being completely ringed by American Liberator airfields, had more than a fair share of these seemingly over-friendly, over-generous expansive servicemen. Natives of Anglia either loved or hated the new arrivals. In the main they were loved by the women, for the gum-chewing, cigar-sucking fellows treated the British females like they'd never been treated before. Gifts of sweets, tinned foods, fine silk underclothes and stockings all cascaded on those lucky enough to shelter beneath the wing of an American serviceman. Local males, either billeted or working in the same area as the Americans, had no chance whatsoever of finding themselves a steady girl friend, for with low pay, no transport (even if they were lucky enough to own a vehicle, petrol was on ration!), and threadbare clothes, what sort of glamorous companion would they make? An apt saying of the time was 'Over-paid, Over-sexed and Over-here!' However, once the ice had been broken and a number of American servicemen taken into East Anglian homes, one could see that the brashness was, in the main, just a cover for shyness. Many tales have been spun about the general gullibility of the American but one of the funniest accounts must surely be the one concerning the memorial in Colne Park close to Colne Engaine in memory of Michael and Philippus Hills. Built by the well-known architect J. Soane, who also designed the Bank of England, it stands over seventy feet high and boasts a handsome copper urn on the upperwork.

American servicemen infested all the local public houses for miles around and soon there developed a kind of friendly feud between the GIs and the locals as the former bent the ear of all and sundry with stories both tall and wild about the good old USA. One evening, an American serviceman enquired what was in the copper urn set way up on top of the column. A local told him, with tongue in cheek, that 'it be filled with liquid gold, that's for sure!'

Nothing else was said, but a couple of nights later the sound of machine-gun fire was heard. Later, it was discovered that the urn was riddled with bullet holes, which can be still seen to this day![1]

[1]*Essex Curiosities*. D.E. Johnson.

German Abwehr agents also had a field day in spreading half truths and malicious gossip and even today, some thirty years later, the stories have grown into a form of folk legend, one of the most popular being the account of strange happenings around the airbase at Rougham. The legend concerns a group of young USAF flyers who, being of German extraction, had refused to fly their bombers over German targets because of the likelihood of dropping bombs on kith or kin. Being grounded until replacement crews could be shipped over from the States, a number of the aircraft were supposed to have been destroyed by acts of sabotage. Even when eventually the bombers did take off on a mission it was reported that several had mysteriously blown up over the Channel. An investigation was carried out, several arrests made and after a drum-head court martial a number of men executed on the spot . . . locals will tell you that their bodies lie buried in Rougham churchyard!

Nearly 100,000 acres of Norfolk farmland was to be taken over by the USAF and by October 1942 the sound of their vibrating aircraft engines from airfields stretching from such places as Debden, Horham, Aldermaston, Wattisham, Duxford, Goxhill, Horsham St Faith, Atcham, Bassingbourn, Tibenham, Bodney and North Pickenham, would disturb the rest of East Anglians during day and night. The building of American airfields was left to the British although it became practice for US engineer batallions to assist with their more sophisticated equipment. A flying field would occupy approximately 500 acres consisting of three concrete runways each 50 yards wide with a main runway of 2,000 yards long. Each airbase was equipped with two independent fuel points capable of taking 144 gallons[1].

First combat operation for the 8th USAF took place on 29 June 1942 when a group of RAF Bostons with American crews flew in a low-level attack on four enemy airfields in the Low Countries. The first American Air Force pilot to fly over Berlin was Jack Jenkins of 38th Squadron, flying his Texas Ranger IV on 3 March 1944.

Whatever the Americans did they always seemed to do it in style: they played big, fought big and even in death they went out in the same style. In the last three years of the war when the 8th USAF was stationed in East Anglia, the best part of 6,000 aircraft and 46,000 men were lost. A visit to their magnificent war cemetery spread out around Maddingley, just outside Cambridge, will bear silent testimony to the tremendous price they paid.

US air activities over and around East Anglia caused far more

---

[1]*The Mighty Eighth*. Roger Freeman.

noise and damage than any actual enemy raids. Aircraft making faulty take-offs had the nasty and unnerving habit of jettisoning their bomb load in the nearest field. Bury St Edmunds had a very near miss along those lines when a bomber ditched its payload nearby. Another near miss was the time when the 491st Group's bomb supply blew up at the Metfield airfield causing grave concern among British authorities as to the potential dangers to those villages and towns situated in the immediate vicinity of USA air bases. With so many bomb-laden aircraft flying day and night missions over war-torn Europe the chances of a major disaster taking place in East Anglia grew daily.

Fears such as these would not have been eased with the news of a drone packed solid with explosives crashing into a wood at Sudbourne Park, Suffolk. The ensuing explosion reduced the timbered area, up to 200 yards away, to a state of matchwood with tree trunks being split in twain as though smitten by a giant axe.

The idea of launching unmanned drone aircraft against strategic enemy positions had culminated after a series of raids against German V1 rocket sites. The first NOBALL (code name for enemy launching sites) missions had taken place over Christmas 1943 when several flights of B-17s and B-24s had unsuccessfully bombed experimental rocket workshops and pads. Frustrated by the abortive attempts to pierce the heavy bulwarks by normal bombing methods USAF authorities had brought into being PROJECT APHRODITE; a scheme which called for an answer to the German V rockets which were being launched from mammoth reinforced concrete structures being built around the Pas de Calais district. The job of stripping out the interiors of B-17 bombers and filling them with over 20,000lb of explosives plus special radio-controlled equipment became a major task of the 562nd Group stationed at Fersfield, Norfolk.

Fersfield was to see a number of such experimental projects launched including the GB-4 television-directed bomb listed under the code name 'Batty'.

In theory the plan was simplicity itself . . . but as with most simple, straightforward plans something hitherto unforeseen nearly always goes wrong. Aphrodite drones were to be launched manually by two volunteer pilots who, after ensuring that the flying bomb was functioning well and on course would throw the fuse control switch and parachute to safety over the Norfolk coastline. A control aircraft flying alongside would then guide the primed bomber to its target.

By 4 August 1944 several drones were ready to be launched from

Fersfield against V1 rocket sites at Watten, Siracourt, Wizernes and Mimojecques. Those that did finally reach their objective did very little damage.

On 12 August two more volunteer pilots prepared to fly their bomb-laden PB4Y Liberator against a target in Heligoland. They were Lieutenant Joseph P. Kennedy (elder brother of the late President John F. Kennedy) and Lieutenant Wilford J. Willis, both serving with the USNR. Once airborne the two pilots took their 21,170lb flying bomb to 15,000 feet and prepared to jump out once over the Blyth estuary. Reaching that point they threw the switch. The 'plane vanished from view with two almighty blasts which reduced their aircraft to pieces no larger than a dinner plate. Extensive damage was caused up to a distance of some five or six miles with 150 damage reports to property being received by the authorities.

A few years ago one of the East Anglian Aircraft Research units managed to locate the engines and parts of the undercarriage which had lain buried for over twenty-five years, returning some of these to the American authorities for metallurgical tests.

Secret missions were also flown from Harrington where the 801st Group delivered arms containers, pigeon hampers, leaflets and espionage agents to behind enemy lines. Over 450 sorties were carried out by this group which had the usual aircraft camouflage replaced by an overall coat of black[1].

By and large the Americans didn't take kindly to East Anglia. By their standards of constant hot water, showers, central heating and air conditioning, mountains of food and drink, plus saloons or bars which never seemed to close, East Anglian Britain was like the outback. The inclement weather conditions which nobody seemed to plan for, plus public houses which closed at 10 pm on the dot, left much to be desired. Their discipline was also rather slipshod and airy-fairy. Very often they would forget a recognition signal which had to be answered when returning from a bombing raid, complaining bitterly when, as they frequently did, the AA gunners opened fire on them. Even as late as 1944 US air-gunners were inclined to be over trigger-happy and uneducated in aircraft recognition, as can be proven when a RAF Beaufighter was shot down over Colchester by a Liberator's tail-gunner.

There was also a tendency for the Americans to grossly exaggerate enemy losses. One occasion springs readily to mind when a raid upon buildings and aircraft at Romilly-sur-Seine was carried out by

[1]*The Mighty Eighth*. Roger Freeman.

Lieutenant Joseph P. Kennedy Junior, USNR, was killed when the aircraft he was piloting – a PB4Y Liberator packed with 21,170 pounds of high explosives – exploded over Norfolk. Based at the US Army Airfield at Winfarthing-Fersfield, Norfolk, Lieutenant Kennedy and Lieutenant Wilford J. Willy had been engaged on a hazardous special mission which was part of the Army-Navy effort to utilise drones (pilotless, radio-controlled aircraft) as an attack weapon against German V2 missile bases. The explosion reduced their aircraft to pieces no larger than a dinner plate. 12 August 1944.

members of VIII B.C. claiming fifty-three enemy aircraft destroyed. Since the war, with unbiased research into existing Luftwaffe records, this figure has now been whittled down to just five.

One cannot deny that the Americans were brave albeit somewhat foolhardy . . . who else but an American would smuggle Prince Bernhard of the Netherlands aboard a bomber of 489th Group and take him for an illicit joy-ride over enemy territory! Some Royal eyebrows were raised at that little incident!

Yet another wild prank involving members of US forces which had far more serious consequences, resulting in the death of a prominent Norfolk landowner, took place on 3 December 1944. At Honingham Hall, just outside Norwich, Sir Eric Teichman – a distinguished traveller, diplomat and expert on Chinese affairs – had just finished lunch when he heard the sound of shooting coming from the direction of his nearby wood. Setting off to investigate he stumbled across a couple of GIs armed with carbines. On challenging them, one of them pointed his weapon at Sir Eric, immediately shooting him dead.

As a result of joint investigations carried out by the US Army Authorities and Norfolk Police, two men were eventually arrested; one, George E. Smith Jnr., of Pittsburgh, being charged with the cold-blooded murder of Sir Eric Teichman.

At a Court Martial held at Attlebridge on 9, 10, 11 and 12 January Smith, aged twenty-seven, was shown to have been a constant source of trouble to the authorities, having already been court-martialled eight times. On the day of the murder Smith, in the company of another GI, Private Leonard S. Wojtacha, had been drinking beer. Breaking into the camp armoury and stealing carbines and ammunition, the two men then decided to go off on a poaching trip to the grounds of Honingham Hall.

Throughout the trial Smith acted cooly, even cockily, with his counsel pleading him Not Guilty by reason of insanity. On 12 January 1945 the eleven officers on the jury delivered a Guilty verdict and Smith was sentenced to death.

Some 600 American bombers also took part in the bombing raid on Dresden of 13, 14 and 15 February 1945 when a grand total of 1,471 tons of high explosives and 1,175 tons of incendiaries reduced the unsuspecting city to rubble and contributed to over 135,000 deaths.

With the invasion of Europe, USAF Groups stationed in East Anglia saw increased activity for they became responsible for airlifting over two million gallons of petrol into France for the advancing Allied invasion force.

For almost a year previous to the actual rocket attacks, RAF Photographic Reconnaissance and Central Interrogation Units had spotted several strange-looking buildings and ski-run structures whilst flying over the Peenemünde district. With the aid of partisan groups working under cover as labourers the Allies had managed to obtain some, although not really enough, limited information on the German secret weapon. The evidence established that almost a hundred ski-sites were nearing completion, and assuming that all of these were operational at the same time, meant that something of the order of two thousand missiles a day could be expected to fall on the British Isles if the Germans were left to complete their programme without interference.

The Germans, who had been experimenting for a number of years with rocket propulsion, had finally perfected a flying bomb which they called FZG.76, Vergeltungswaffe 1 (Reprisal Weapon No. 1) hence the V1. In Germany it became known as the *Kirschkern* or cherry stone. Weighing approximately two tons – with a warhead less than half that amount – its overall length was 25ft with a wingspan of 16ft.

Despite all manner of strange speculative rumours the V1 was not radio-controlled, being powered by a pulse-jet which was operational for about one hour using low-grade aviation spirit. Its range was in the region of 150 miles, later to be increased to 250 miles. Rockets launched from sites in Holland could, and did, strike parts of London, although a great number fell in East Anglia.

The first four VIs to be fired against England were launched on 13 June 1944 and by the 15th well over one hundred rockets had landed on the east coast with one, thought to be meant for Greater London, landing way up in Norfolk.

For those who had been through the earlier air-raids of 1941-42 this new horror was to prove a little disquieting. During the blitz they had been able to see and hear the enemy as he flew overhead, knowing that there was a good chance if British fighters didn't get him, the AA guns might. With the Doodle-Bug (one of many pet names dreamt up for Hitler's secret weapon) all one could hope and pray for was that the motor didn't cut out when immediately overhead. If it did then all one could do was dive beneath something solid and pray, for the V1 had a very nasty habit of crash-diving once the fuel supply had been automatically cut off. Although the actual number of people killed by flying bombs was less than one for every missile which crossed the water or came within range of the defences, the area of superficial damage was so wide and the effect on peoples' nerves so alarming that crowded towns once more saw an exodus of frightened evacuees making for the countryside out west. This time it was not just mothers and children who fled; fathers fearing for the safety and welfare of their families packed bag and baggage, moving the entire home contents.

On 16 June the Ministry of Home Security issued the following statement: 'When the engine of the pilotless aircraft stops and the light at the end of the machine is seen to go out it may mean that explosion will soon follow.'

The flying bomb had arrived! Strange to think that such an eminent personage as the Prime Minister's Scientific Adviser Lord Cherwell, or Professor Lindemann, to give him his old alien name, had thought that the idea of the Germans building long range rockets was a load of rubbish[1]. He had even advised Churchill so.

A lot of East Anglians remember those flying bombs all too well, for over a stretch of the Essex coast dubbed 'Doodle-Bug Alley' one could see flights of the putt-putting monsters making their noisy way towards the big cities. A Mr H. Burgess recalls the time when, doing a fire-watching stint on the roof of an Eastern National Bus Garage at around 5 am, he was nearly run down by a flying bomb. He had taken up his position when he suddenly noticed one of the VIs heading straight for him. Flying at about 50-60 feet above ground level the roaring missile zipped just over his head . . . so close in fact that he could smell the acrid exhaust fumes.

The true function of the *Vergeltungswaffe 1* warfare was, as the name implied, a retaliatory measure against the increased Allied bombing of civilian targets in Germany. A protest by Bishop Bell of Chichester raised in the House of Lords during February 1944 questioning the moral legality of this practice was played down by Winston Churchill.

To combat the number of flying bombs that were being launched against vulnerable and very often undefended targets, a special Gun Belt known as a 'Diver Strip' was introduced along the east coast. At one time a Gun Belt was thrown up between Yarmouth and Clacton, while during the 16-19 September more guns were moved into the Harwich-Clacton area. Planned by Lieutenant-General Sir Frederick Pile, the idea was to shift this 'Diver Strip' to whatever section of the coast was in line with flights of incoming rockets. It was aided by a web of high-flying barrage balloon and RAF fighters, who either machine-gunned the V1s down or failing that, flew alongside

[1] *The Battle of the V Weapons 1944-1945*. Basil Collier.

the rocket trying to waggle their wingtips under the enemy aircraft to throw it off course and back out to sea. Five fighter pilots died whilst trying to perform the latter trick. The idea of the Gun Belt meant that if fighter 'planes didn't stop the rockets then on no account was an aircraft allowed to follow the enemy into a 'Diver Strip', for once in that area both rocket and 'plane would be met with a blanket of concentrated artillery fire.

Brigadier J.A.E. Burls was responsible for producing a portable gun platform popularly called the 'Pile Mattress', which saved weeks of construction work and vast quantities of steel and concrete.

During the summer of 1944 gun and balloon installations would account for eight to ten V1s a day while twelve fighter squadrons accounted for another thirty a day; but even so fifty rockets a day were falling on Greater London and the outskirts.

'I was working in a field near the marshes when I first saw those strange things rising into the air . . . they looked for all the world like stars going straight up into the sky until I lost sight of them. They left a distinct vapour trail behind them.' Thus spoke Mr S. Lummis, who had been a farm worker at Beaumont, Essex, just after witnessing the launching of the new, far more deadly rocket, the V2, or as the Germans called it, A-4.

On 25 September a rocket which was to become known as the V2 was launched against targets at Ipswich and Norwich . . . one missile fell at Hoxne, Suffolk. During the next three weeks the enemy battery situated at Staveren, Friesland, dispatched forty-three rockets but fortunately neither target was reached apart from one that landed just outside Norwich city limits. A number of near misses were registered with superficial damage being done to the Dereham Road and Mile Cross area while on another occasion the Hellesdon Golf Course found itself with a new bunker when a V2 exploded nearby. But Norwich City itself was spared . . . fate had decreed otherwise.

At first the anxious authorities kept the news of the new rocket very secret indeed. ARP reports referred to the A-4 as 'Big Ben', a very apt description when one sees the actual size of the thing. In the end however, they did release a few restricted details.

The A-4, or V2, whichever you like to call it, was at long last an honest-to-goodness rocket, something the Germans had been striving to perfect for so long. The brainchild of Walter Dornberger and Dr Wernher von Braun, it carried approximately nine tons of ethyl alcohol, water and liquid oxygen, was armed with a one ton warhead containing 1,650 lbs of explosives, and weighed altogether nearly thirteen tons. Its maximum range was 200 miles rising to a height of sixty miles at the peak of its trajectory. When striking a target this missile had a tendency to bury its head into the ground when exploding, scattering debris over an area of some 600 yards and leaving a shallow crater 4ft by about 27ft in diameter.

A special Radar watch with series of stations stretching from Lowestoft to Dover aimed at pin-pointing rockets launched from Europe was introduced. At one point it was planned to increase the AA barrage along the coastal strip in a desperate attempt to blast rockets out of the sky as they passed overhead. Fortunately the whole idea was shelved owing to the possibility of general alarm and damage to people and property which would have been caused by the falling shrapnel.

During their short lifespan a grand total of 1,115 rockets landed on Great Britain with 400 of these falling on the county of Essex.

During this period a series of intensive search and destroy operations were evolved by the RAF against the V2 sites. On one of these, on 14 February 1945, a Flight Lieutenant Raymond Baxter[1]

Raymond Baxter (second left) Commander of A Flight 602 (City of Glasgow) Squadron, at a briefing prior to a raid on a V2 rocket site.

[1]Presenter of many of the B.B.C.s *Tomorrow's World* Series.

commanding A Flight 602 (City of Glasgow) Squadron, stationed at RAF Coltishall, led a flight of Spitfire XVIs against a target situated in wooded dunes a few miles north of The Hague. After attacking the site several times the airmen were somewhat taken aback to see, rising out of the woods in full majestic take-off, the gleaming body of a V2 rocket! One pilot, Flight Sergeant 'Cupid' Love, found he had the monster right in line with his gun-sight and blasted off a few rounds. As Raymond Baxter observed later: 'Thank goodness he didn't hit anything vital or we wouldn't be here today to tell the tale.'

The last V2 rocket to reach the shores of the UK fell at Orpington, Kent, on 27 March 1945, at 4.45 pm. The last flying bomb to be launched from a *ground site* against England was on 1 September 1944. After that period they relied solely on air-launching. The last flying bomb to approach the UK was brought down by AA gunfire off Orfordness on 29 March at 12.43 pm[1].

The dreaded V2 rocket, Germany's secret weapon launched against Britain during World War II.

[1]*The Battle of the V Weapons 1944-1945.* Basil Collier.

And so the Blitz had finished, bringing death and destruction to all walks of life.

Today, some thirty-odd years after the end of the conflict, we are still digging up unexploded bombs and shells along East Anglian cliff faces; the odd mine or two is dislodged to bring instant panic and, for those old enough to remember, a touch of wartime nostalgia. In Essex alone there fell during the 1939-45 period something in the region of . . .

13,792 high explosive bombs.
1,498 'Butterfly' bombs[1].
680 oil bombs.
142,000 incendiaries.
528 parachute mines (106 of which failed to explode).
511 flying bombs (V1s).
400 long range rockets (V2s).

These caused 845 deaths and 5,979 injured.

[1] A small bomb resembling a one pint paint tin which during its downward flight sprouted a pair of tin wings making it look like a butterfly.

CHAPTER SIX

COASTAL VIGIL

When it comes to the important matter of defence the East Anglian coastline has always proved to be one of Britain's weakest points. From the earliest times we have reports of marauding bands of pirates and free-traders pillaging and plundering this stretch of coastline with impunity, meeting little or no organised resistance. In Elizabethan times we learn of a series of watch towers and beacons being erected along the cliff-tops from which signal fires could be lit if and when an enemy was seen approaching from the sea. In the eighteenth and nineteenth centuries, during the Napoleonic Wars, a complex system of fortifications known as Martello Towers was built along our coastline. During the First World War these towers were reinforced by building pill-boxes, observation posts and heavy gun emplacements alongside. However, the enemy by then had no need to come within range of these weapons for his long-range guns could launch a barrage well outside their striking distance across the Channel. Such was the case on 14 January 1918 when a German bombardment sent fifty to sixty shells whistling into Yarmouth, which was a fishing centre in those days, all within a period of seven minutes, killing seven and wounding many more. This was followed up on the windswept night of the 25th by yet another bombardment by Imperial German light-draft naval vessels firing sixty-eight shells and two star-shells against Southwold, one of the star-shells falling at Easton and the other at Chilvers Farm, extensive damage being done to Iona Cottage and the Summer House . . . truly the writing was on the wall!

Docks and harbours had to be protected and on the outbreak of the Second World War men of the National Defence Corps, a specially trained band of men, took to guarding Naval Oil Storage Tanks and pipe-lines against sabotage attempts. Among other points Felixstowe, Ipswich and Harwich saw men of the NDC in attendance.

At the popular resort of Southend the pier was taken over by the Royal Navy on 25 August 1939 just a few days before World War II was declared, becoming HQ for the Thames & Medway Control. Southend, in fact, became the assembly point for East Coast Convoys, with masters of ships that joined the convoys using the famous pier as a briefing point. The period between 1939-45 saw some 3,367 convoys, consisting of 84,297 ships rendezvousing there[1]. Across the estuary between Shoeburyness and the coast of Kent a giant defence boom was built. This was primarily intended to prevent enemy submarines or fast-moving motor torpedo boats from entering the vulnerable, vital position.

One of the first major tragic losses of the war was the sinking of *HMS Gipsy* on the evening of Tuesday 21 November 1939. At about 9.23 pm an enemy seaplane was heard approaching *HMS Badger* (name given to the Harwich Naval Base) and dropped what later turned out to be a magnetic mine. After machine-gunning the area it flew off. *HMS Gipsy*, together with the *Boadicea* and the Polish ship *Burza*, set off in the inky-blackness of the unlit harbour to investigate the disturbance. Just inside Landguard Point the *Gipsy* ran foul of the mine, being ripped open by the ensuing explosion. Sinking within minutes she took some fifty crew-members to a watery grave. A Special Constable, Leslie M. Petch, who had been on patrol along the seafront, recalls seeing a host of searchlights playing about the icy waters as small craft plied back and forth to rescue the survivors. The one outstanding thing he poignantly remembers was the feeling of absolute helplessness as he watched the men splashing, kicking, screaming and drowning in the muddy harbour waters. 'I was so close to them that I felt as though I could just reach out with my hand and pluck them to safety, but barbed-wire defences and steep harbour walls spelt out the futility of such action.'

Another early wartime loss was that of the *Ocean Lassie*, an examination vessel which went to the bottom within one minute after being struck by a parachute mine. Out of her original crew of thirteen only six were rescued.

Defending the East Anglian coast called for several extreme measures including the drastic action of blowing gaps in a number of piers to thwart enemy landings. This hasty, single-minded action caused something of a problem to several lifeboat crews who found themselves cut off from their boats and equipment. At Walton, Clacton, Felixstowe and Cromer the sappers had blown several holes in the piers. At Clacton the pier had been breached without any warning whatsoever while the lifeboat *Edward Z. Dresden* was still in her boathouse. Extensive damage was caused to both boat and equipment causing the station to be closed for a couple of months while the boat was taken to Rowhedge for repairs. Later she was to operate from Brightlingsea for three months before returning to Clacton pier after the gap had been suitably bridged.

[1]*Wreck and Rescue on the Essex Coast*, Robert Malster.

Above: Rusty remains of beach defences built along the Suffolk coast during the 1939-40 period.
Below: Remains of coastal defences constructed along the Suffolk coast to protect East Anglia against the threatened Germany invasion during the 1939-45 war.

Right from the very beginning of the war the lifeboat service had seen considerable action on the high seas. Between September 1939 and April 1940, 135 British merchant ships and 143 neutral vessels were sunk in waters around the British coasts[1]. During the first nine months of hostilities Britain's lifeboats were launched 315 times but in the last twelve weeks as the 'phoney war' gave way to the real thing they were launched 370 times, helping to save 895 shipwrecked souls and thirty-nine vessels. The first wartime call by any British lifeboat in the British Isles was that carried out by Aldeburgh No 1 lifeboat when called out to tend the stricken 8,640-ton liner *Magdapur* which was sunk by enemy action off the Suffolk coast during the first week of the war. Crew members saved numbered eighteen Europeans and fifty-six lascars. Six men were lost, and it took two-and-half hours to clean out the congealed blood and oil.

The first major setback for the British was the disaster of Dunkirk when German armour pushed the badly mauled and exhausted BEF down to the water's edge. Much has been written and screened about this particular phase of the war and East Anglia certainly played an important part in the rescue operation. When the call went out on 30 May 1940 for all available shipping both large and small to strike out for the French coast the immediate response was enormous. Lifeboats were especially to the fore; being the *Louise Stephens* of Lowestoft, *Mary Scott* of Southwold, *Abdy Beauclerk* & *Lucy Lawes* of Aldeburgh, the *E.M.E.D* of Walton & Frinton, *Edward Z. Dresden* of Clacton, *Greater London* (Civil Service No. 3), Southend-on-Sea, *Charles Dibdin* of Walmer and the new, unnamed lifeboat just completed at the Rowhedge Iron Works, Essex.

Although the lifeboat crews delivered their boats to the agreed meeting point at Dover they were in fact manned by Royal Navy personnel after a heated argument with the coxswains of Hythe, Walmer and Dungeness lifeboats. In a nutshell, the naval authorities had refused to furnish written details of pensions likely to be awarded to the families of those crew-members killed or maimed in the ensuing action. They (the coxswain and crews) refused to sail for Dunkirk unless such warranty was forthcoming . . . the outcome culminating in the lifeboats being manned by naval personnel and the disappointed and disgruntled lifeboatmen shipped back to their home stations[2].

Both Clacton and Walton lifeboats worked in Dunkirk Harbour. The Walton 'boat was dive-bombed by German aircraft on the way to the French coast, the officer-in-charge being killed by a cannon

[1] *Saved from the Sea*, Robert Malster.
[2] *Storm on the Waters*, Charles Vince, page 36.

shell; fouling her propellor shaft she managed to limp home to Dover where it was cut away by a diver. She then returned to France for the rest of the evacuation. Because of this increasing problem with fouled ropes a towing-rope made from coconut fibre which floated, causing less risk of fouling the propellors, was introduced.

Southend's lifeboat *Greater London*, manned by a naval crew, also saw action at Dunkirk harbour and at the very end of the evacuation saved the *HMS Kellett* which was trying to evacuate some 200 French soldiers. Unfortunately the warship's screws became entangled in some of the debris floating about the harbour and could not budge an inch. It was at this point that the *Greater London* hove into sight fully laden to the water line with a cargo of exhausted soldiers. Noticing the *Kellet's* predicament she took a line aboard and dragged the ensnared ship free and off into deep water.

Leading Seaman Ernest Johnson, who served aboard *HMS Clacton*, a Fleet Minesweeper. He bore a charmed life, narrowly escaping death on a number of occasions. Luck was with him when the *Clacton* struck a mine off Bastia Harbour in 1943, killing thirty-three men out of a crew of seventy.

The lifeboats were not alone in this stirring chapter of British history, for a general flotilla of ships gathered around Dunkirk to ferry off the waiting men. Many of the owners insisted upon accompanying their little craft across the Channel even though they had little or no sea experience; a number even being lost by a deadly hail of bullets and bombs dropped by harrying enemy aircraft.

By 4 June 338,226 troops had been rescued – 225,000 of these being British. Among the great loss of equipment could be included 600 tanks and over 2,000 guns and 13,000 men.

One East Anglian man to be rescued from Dunkirk was Mr Joe Pusey. Serving as a regular soldier with the 2nd Batt. Royal Fusiliers he fought with a rear-guard party from the Albert Canal, Belgium, through to Dunkirk. He recounts how his regiment was completely out-manoeuvred by the Germans on all fronts. Once on the outskirts of Dunkirk Joe was ordered to hold a position with the aid of an anti-tank rifle. He had been assured that it would stop anything the Germans cared to offer. He remembers the effects of his first shot at an advancing motorcycle combination. Taking aim at approximately 300 yards the missile did no more than bounce off the sidecar like a pea off a toy drum! Without any more ado the Germans spun their machine about and made off in the opposite direction. Joe didn't have to wait very long however, for a few minutes afterwards he heard the all-too-familiar crump of mortar fire. Waiting for a change in the fire pattern he made for the cover of a hedge and ran like the blazes. Although wounded and eventully taken prisoner he managed to make good his escape under cover of darkness and make his way back to the beach, where he was lucky enough to find a space aboard a crowded ship which managed to limp back to British shores.

Once the tired, hungry men had been landed it was the work of the waiting women to feed them and tend the wounded. They slept wherever they could find a space to lie, being so exhausted that many didn't even feel the gentle touch as blistered bleeding feet were washed. To get the men away from coastal disembarkation points the railways were formed into a common pool of coaching stock with over 186 trains being utilised for the evacuation of rescued troops. Code named 'Operation Dynamo', a total of 319,116 troops in 620 trains were worked away from the disembarkation points to reception areas in all parts of the country, the whole of the movement being performed in sixteen days[1].

If the lifeboat crews hadn't had the satisfaction of actually being at Dunkirk they certainly made up for it once the boats had been

[1]*The LMS at War*, George C. Nash.

returned to their rightful owners. As one reads the log of exciting actions one wonders just how they came through it all intact. It was not just the dangers of the deep that they faced, for one great hazard was that of launching the boats without floodlights. In the early days of the war even the use of wireless was forbidden in case of listening submarines. Maroons were also forbidden, so crew-members were mustered by a system of messengers mounted on cycles.

Sometimes several lifeboats would be called out to the same distress call. Such was the case on 6 August 1941 when six ships from a passing convoy ran aground on the storm-swept Happisburgh sandbanks. The Navy called upon Cromer, Gorleston, Lowestoft and Sheringham lifeboats to assist. Great Yarmouth assisted in the actual rescue, but the Sheringham boat (twenty miles away) and Lowestoft (twenty-five miles) arrived too late. It took three hours to rescue 119 men.

As the enemy stepped up his activities around East Anglia a danger area to British shipping was that nick-named 'E-Boat Alley', this being a stretch of water which ran between Happisburgh Sands and the Norfolk coast eight miles away. Here, fast German E-boats would lurk, waiting to pounce on slow-moving convoys. Time and time again when men of the RNLI answered the call of distress they did so at a terrible risk for the lifeboats were literally defenceless, setting out armed with just a couple of service rifles and fifty rounds of ammunition. It is recorded that these were never used once in anger except to explode runaway sea-mines. These men and boats undertook various tasks from helping the Home Guard with mock invasion exercises, taking food and supplies when none could be got through, ferrying doctors to the injured, and men from bomb-disposal units to inspect mine or bomb damage as well as countless other tasks. Apart from routine rescues and keeping an eye on the steel fortresses which had been erected to guard the North Sea approaches, it is interesting to note that certain members of the Clacton lifeboat helped with experiments for the War Office. In May 1943 Coxswain Charles Ellis and Commander Tansley set out aboard a boat loaded with experimental apparatus together with its inventor, Dr. A. Klein, a Jewish refugee who had escaped from Austria at the beginning of the war. This simple piece of equipment was to save the lives of many 'ditched' airmen, for with this tiny still complete with full directions of use the distressed men could distil enough seawater to last them until they were rescued. Comment at the time by Coxswain Ellis: 'Rather flat and tasteless – but certainly had no trace of seawater.'

During the Battle of Britain the lifeboat service found itself called out to rescue both enemy and allied shot-down airmen. The Walton and Frinton *E.M.E.D.* was called out five times in 1940 and seven in 1941 to crashed aircraft. In one incident they found a dead German pilot floating upright supported by his lifejacket. Up at Sheringham it was the landlord of a seafront public house who happened to be standing by the window cleaning glasses when he spotted a dark speck bobbing about some two miles out to sea. It turned out to be a rubber dinghy with five Polish airmen aboard. They had been afloat without food for some seventeen hours.

Age didn't seem to be a barrier to the men of the RNLI for the oldest serving wartime lifeboatman was Coxswain Henry Blogg of Cromer who at the prime age of sixty-five was aboard the *H.F. Bailey* when she spent nine hours assisting with the famous Happisburgh Sands rescue of 6/7 August 1941. For this he was to receive the third service clasp to his Gold Medal as well as the British Empire Medal.

With the introduction of the Second Front and the invasion of Europe in 1944 and with transport and glider forces being built up, more than 75% of disaster calls answered by Anglian lifeboats involved aircrews and aircraft which had fallen foul of the sea. Working in close harmony with the RNLI were the Air Sea Rescue Launches which were stationed at Wells and Gorleston. This force had a special task during the latter stages of the war involving the tracking and rescue of a special airborne lifeboat which could be carried beneath the fuselage of specially adapted aircraft and dropped by parachutes to men drifting in rubber dinghies. They were fitted with small petrol engines and sails plus radio and a store of vital supplies.

Being a lone island Great Britain depends greatly on her freeway of the seas which surround her coasts. When the Germans started to lay sea-mines in the Channel it began to prove a major headache for the British naval authorities. When magnetic mines started to be dropped by parachute in the Thames and Harwich harbour on the night of 21 November 1939 a magnetic sweep had to be quickly introduced. This took the form of a forty-foot long wooden skid which was drawn behind a ship. Around the eight-inch high pegs was wound a heavy electric cable which in turn was linked to a generator aboard the towing vessel. The generator was to keep a surge of power passing through the coil thus ensuring a fairly safe passage through the magnetic mine fields. A number of these skids were built at the

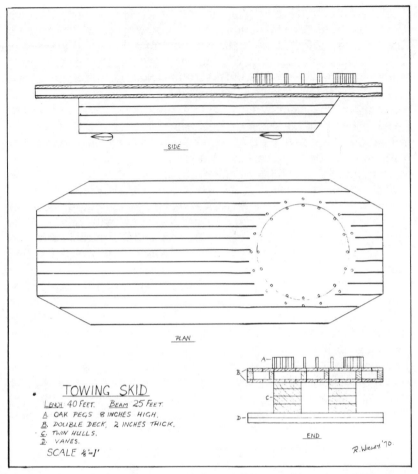

Drawing of a wooden towing-skid built at Wivenhoe shipyard to sweep magnetic mines dropped around the East Anglian coast during 1940.

Wivenhoe Ship Yards, where later the wooden mine sweepers were built. These ships, resembling the famous Yarmouth drifter, pulled a double-longitudinal sweep through which a surge of current was passed, thus causing the mines to be exploded. Every minute a pulse of 3,000 amperes was sent through the cables, which was sufficient to explode all the magnetic mines on the sea-bottom over an area of more than ten acres. Although the skids and sweeps answered the purpose for which they were first intended they were in fact a very impractical piece of equipment. Foul weather, floating debris and lack of manoeuvreability soon saw these aids replaced by mine-sweepers equipped with de-gaussing coils which were wrapped around the hull above the water-line. These did not explode the mines but demagnetized them leaving them relatively harmless. By the end of May 1940, 2,000 merchant ships and 1,704 warships had been fitted with de-gaussing coils[1].

The chance to examine the workings of the magnetic mine materialized when a mine was observed to fall into tidal water off Shoeburyness. Lt.-Cdr. G.W. Ouvry of *HMS Vernon* and Dr. A.B. Wood of the Naval Mine Design Department were shipped at once to investigate the object. When the tide had fallen sufficiently enough to reveal the parachute a working party of soldiers dragged the mine to low water. During the course of the day another mine was discovered nearby. Non-magnetic tools of brass for dismantling the mine were designed and made locally and after being taken to pieces the detonator, primer release, primer and hydrostatic clock and fuse were taken to Naval Mine Design Department for examination. Among the few men to work on the magnetic mine was Lionel Hawkins, RNVR – a descendant of John Hawkins of Elizabethan fame. He, together with his assistant Mr G. Goss, were killed while examining a mine at Walton-on-Naze.

American 'Lease-Lend' Ships. 180 B.Y.M.S. This minesweeper was capable of sixteen knots, powered by a twin-screw Diesel Electric. Armaments consisted of 1,3 inch gun at the bows and 2,20 mm. Oerlikon guns port and starboard on the bridge. *Photo: Imperial War Museum.*

[1]*Science at War*, J.G. Crowther & R. Whiddington

One of the major mine-sweeper bases in East Anglia was at the ancient fishing town of Brightlingsea, Essex. From this snug little harbour the sweepers could slip out to clear the East Coast waters. It is interesting to note that the popular myth of rum-soaked sailors clinging to a sea-swept bridge was sadly shattered when a local newspaper reported:

'Six firms were fined £23 each for selling over their allowed quota of milk. The Ministry of Food has set out regulations rationing milk to two pints per week per customer. The Brightlingsea firms accused pleaded that "The medical authorities ought to be pleased to think that members of the WRNS and merchant seamen are drinking so much milk at Brightlingsea." '

Bureaucracy being bureaucracy it didn't come as a surprise to read in the same newspaper just a week later that as much as fifteen gallons of milk a day were being tipped down a drain at a nearby farm at Arlesford . . . just because the Ministry hadn't been to collect it!

A great number of ships were built at Wivenhoe and Brightlingsea, mainly being constructed of wood. With each ship taking on average something like 250 trees for its construction it was reckoned that areas up to a radius of some twenty-five miles were decimated of elm and oak trees. These shipyards came under the grading of 'protected places' and 'key points'. The building programme included 129 landing craft of various types, eight 35ft fast motor-boats, fifteen

Seaman Gunner C.J. Singleton shown here testing a 20 mm. Oerlikon gun aboard one of the American 'Lease-Lend' mine-sweepers. Nearly 1,000 of these 'sweepers were built in the USA and brought back by men stationed at Lowestoft.

towing skids, six 32ft cutters, five 30ft motor-pinnaces, eight 25ft motor-cutters, four 25ft fast cutters, six 52½ft steam pinnaces, forty-nine 16ft fast dinghies, forty-one 18ft G.S. dinghies, six 60ft G.S. pinnaces, eight 60ft A.S.R. pinnaces, thirty-two 45ft refuellers, twenty-nine 40ft seaplane tenders, forty-six airborne lifeboats, five 50ft refuellers, twenty-four 36ft harbour launches and 4,641 bridging pontoons. Wivenhoe can also lay claim to building certain sections of the giant pre-fabricated Mulberry Harbours used with great success in the invasion of Normandy.

Britain's thriving fishing industry was also to suffer badly during the war for not only did trawlermen have to contend with the dangers of runaway sea-mines, machine-gun and bombing raids, and the hazards of uncharted wrecks or floating debris, but numerous restrictions curtailed their work endlessly. One popular wartime yarn spun around the waterfront pubs of Brightlingsea relates how, during the early part of the war when boats were not allowed out past a certain point, one boat on an illicit midnight fishing trip trawled up a half-decomposed body full of eels. When one of the younger men enquired what they should do with the remains, his older, wiser companion answered, 'Nothing . . . chuck it back where we found it!' The next night the men returned to haul in the float-marked corpse which was packed full of eels again. This was to go on for several nights yielding the same bonus until wind and tide changed, sweeping the grisly remains out into deeper water.

It wasn't just the fishing boats alone which fell target to marauding aircraft, for between 1940-44 Yarmouth, which was then a fishing town, was to suffer ninety-seven air raids; up to November 1941 that ancient watering-place had had seventy-two raids causing 110 deaths and damaging 11,500 homes.

East Anglian-based barges carrying vital supplies also ran the gauntlet of bomb and bullet while the famous cross-channel railway steamers requisitioned for Government service were defensively armed and painted with the now all-so-familiar Admiralty grey. They were called upon to act as assault ships, boom defence craft, mine-layers and mine-sweepers, and hospital carriers as well as military transport.

Above: A derelict concrete barge lying off Walton-on-Naze backwaters – once part of a massive supply convoy sent out to Normandy during the invasion of Europe in 1944.
Below: Some of the damage caused by the air raids over Yarmouth.

Typical bomb devastation to private property in Yarmouth.

CHAPTER SEVEN

STRICTLY HUSH-HUSH

War, with all its paraphernalia and majesty of uniforms, marching troops and bands, convoys of speeding vehicles or flights of noisy aircraft, would indeed be nothing without the brains of the scientist. From earliest times when one particular thinking Man discovered that throwing a sharp flint tied to the end of a stick was far superior to belting your enemy at close quarters with a lump of stone, the antagonistic Homo sapiens has wrestled and schemed with various ways to overthrow a stronger enemy or prey.

Around East Anglia ancient man used to knap flint axes, knives and spear heads as can be witnessed by the evidence of a Flint Industry established during the Early Hoxnian period (about 250,000 BC) at Jaywick, Essex. Much later, during the early nineteenth century, Harwich was to see more sophisticated secret experiments carried out in the name of War. *Ipswich Journal*, 19 October 1811:

> Another plan, of the most destructive nature, is now in agitation, and has been brought forward by a Mr Fane; and was a few days since exhibited before the Lords of the Admiralty. It is a four-pound shot, wrapped around with prepared cotton, and made very hard, so as to appear like a large cannon shot; it presents one solid mass of fire and whatever it hits, whether rigging or hull of ship, will immediately take fire.

And again on Saturday 7 December 1811:

> An experiment was lately made on board the *Victory*, Sir J. Savmarez's flagship, of discharging guns without the use of fire; it was produced by a slight pressure of the fingers on a prepared tube put into the vent of the gun; the effect was instantaneous and certain, and completely prevented the accidents that so frequently happen in action from the loose powder that is spilt on the decks. It is the invention of Captain Manby of Yarmouth.

By the twentieth century warfare had progressed with such gigantic strides that poor Captain Manby would have indeed wondered what had happened to his 'magic tube'!

With the end of World War I those thinking few in high Governmental departments recognised that war was no longer a struggle of brute strength alone. The submarine, wireless, fighter and bomber 'planes and advancement in the field of armaments and explosives had revealed that, to stand a chance of winning the next major conflict, scientific know-how would have to be backed to the hilt. British scientists had learnt a painful lesson during the 1914-18 war when German Zeppelins and Gotha bombers had flown over the British Isles to drop their bombs with near impunity. What was needed, and needed in a hurry, was a method of detecting the presence of enemy aircraft *before* they got to the East Coast.

With the foundation of the Third German Reich in 1933 Hitler began to construct a huge air force as part of his rearmament programme. The Air Ministry saw this force as an immediate threat, for Britain was indeed within easy range, and they anxiously considered whether any new ways of meeting the threat could be found. The multiplication of existing weapons was not enough, for the future enemy had a preponderance of industrial productive power. Could our scientists provide something completely advanced that would offset the Germans' numerical advantages and give adequate protection to the towns and cities of Britain where the mass of the population lives and necessary materials of war and life must be manufactured?

In October 1934 Dr H.E. Wimperis, the Director of Scientific Research at the Air Ministry, and a colleague, Mr A.P. Rowe, reviewed the many ways in which science might be utilised for such a purpose. The outcome was a Committee of Research on Air Defence under the chairmanship of Mr H.T. Tizard.

By now the press were clamouring for a secret weapon to be developed . . . why not a death ray? The public took up this cry and soon everyone was gossiping that such a wonder-ray had indeed been perfected. In January 1935 Wimperis had indeed consulted Watson Watt, the Superintendent of the Radio Department of the National Physical Laboratory, to see if such a ray was at all feasible or possible. It was shown that the quantity of energy needed to upset an engine or hurt a person was far too great to be provided by any known method . . . *but that the quantity of energy needed to detect the presence of aeroplanes or other objects might reasonably be produced by an extension of known means*[1].

Soon Watson Watt had been given the green light to go ahead with his experiments and on 26 February he was able to demonstrate with the aid of a small van packed full of suitable radio receivers the tracking of a lone aircraft some eight miles away. By 13 May a special laboratory had been built at Orford Ness, a quiet, lonely spot on the Suffolk coast. In June the Tizard Committee visited the laboratory and were suitably impressed when an aircraft was tracked

[1] *Science at War*, J.G. Crowther & R. Whiddington.

for more than forty miles. By March 1939 rapid improvements had been made to the equipment which was moved to larger premises at Bawdsey Manor, near Felixstowe. Here, aerial towers of 250 feet high were constructed, culminating in tracking an aircraft flying at over 1,500 feet and a distance of seventy-five miles.

The observers at Bawdsey noted with ease the movement of aircraft over the neighbouring areas of the North Sea and could follow more closely the arrival and landfall of airlines from the Continent than the controller at Croydon Airport. One disturbing factor did, however, emerge during their observations: Deutsche Lufthansa aircraft nearly always tended to fly low over Bawdsey whenever they approached or left England! (Their suspicions were indeed correct . . . see page 146.)

Air exercises were held during September 1936 and by May 1937 Royal Air Force officers were being trained to use the Bawdsey apparatus for fighting operations and this was to become the prototype of a chain of stations erected to cover the Thames Estuary. Preparations for the construction of some twenty watch towers, their rays covering the coast and forty miles seawards, were then started. It seemed that the ideal site was set well back from the sea and with a smooth approach down to the sea. Hills and high bluffs were to be avoided at all costs for these had a tendency to send back permanent radio echoes which in turn overlapped and masked signals from approaching aircraft. By the time Mr Chamberlain was to leave for his Munich meeting in September 1938 over £2,000,000 had been spent on the secret weapon and the east coast of Britain was cloaked by invisible radio waves. Aircraft approaching at a height of 15,000 feet were detected by them more than 100 miles away through rain or cloud, night or fog. Even their exact numbers could be counted and evading tactics observed and logged.

For East Anglians at any rate, the magic 'death ray' had at last been perfected . . . or so they believed. Rumours flourished wildly in those early experimental radar days as folk speculated on just what was being developed by the 'Islanders' at their lonely outpost on the Suffolk coast. Some motorists complained that vehicles approaching the Bawdsey area suffered engine failure as invisible rays affected their electrical circuits. Others claimed that light aircraft had dropped like stones, also with engine failure, when flying over the radar station. When the station had been based at Orford Ness fishermen spending the day off that part of the coast complained that exposed parts of their bodies were being blistered by the rays. Just what kind of secret experiments were carried out along that stretch of coast we may never find out for even today, some forty years after the installation of the post, a veil of secrecy surrounds the Bawdsey-Shingle Street area. At the Ministry of Defence lies a thick file indexed 'Evacuation of civil population from the village of Shingle Street, East Suffolk' . . . plus a seventy-five year ban on the publication of its contents.

At the beginning of the war inhabitants of some twenty cottages were forced to leave their homes and were evacuated to nearby Hollesley, leaving their village as a proving ground for experimental work carried out by both British and American armaments experts.

Left: Sole remaining steel mast built at the remote Great Bromley radar station. *Right:* Wartime photograph of a radar aerial mounted on top of the ancient 1796 Trinity House tower at Walton-on-Naze, Essex.

One semi-official source – a member of MI9 – suggests that it was on the cards that early atomic missiles had been tested around the Orford Beach area. Interviewing former wartime officers of the local police and coast guard revealed that they knew something but refused to divulge any information, knowing that they too were still bound by the Official Secrets Act. One slim clue, however, came from Miss Pierce Butler of Seckford Street, near Woodbridge, who during the war paid a visit to her cousin Lady Prestige of Bourne Park, Canterbury. Also staying at Bourne Park as a guest of Lady Prestige was Air Commodore Patrick Huskin who was involved in the development of secret armaments. Although blind (the outcome of a bomb accident), Huskin had been kept on with the Department, working by touch alone. During the course of her stay Miss Butler very often accompanied the Air Commodore on fishing trips to the nearby lake; she acting as his rower and guide. Learning that she originated from the village of Shingle Street he chanced to remark that certain tests of a very important nature were being carried out there on a new revolutionary type of bomb . . . one that could change the course of the war.

Now reverted to a sleepy seaside village popularised by fishermen in search of a spot of beach fishing, the giant radar masts have started to be demolished to make way for a 'Bloodhound' missile site.

Travellers using the A604 Harwich to Colchester main road will hardly fail to notice the towering steel mast as they pass the Great Bromley turn-off. This is all that remains of the original three radar masts that were erected on this spot during the early days of the war. Initially a group of wooden masts had been built near this site off Honey Pot Lane but these, proving unsuitable, had to be demolished with explosive charges. The entire area is honey-combed with deep underground bunkers and shelters which during those wartime days accommodated radar personnel and stores.

One former Special Police Constable, Frederick Dansie, was part of a team responsible for patrolling a fourteen-mile area, allowing nobody into the restricted zone unless they carried a special pass issued by the authorities. He recalls that one storm-bound winter's night – while sheltering in a local pub doorway – he stumbled over a bulky briefcase which had been left against the doorstep. Inside were plans, maps and blueprints of the entire coastal radar network. If they had fallen into the wrong hands the enemy would have indeed had a field day!

Coastal defence being all-important, no effort was spared in reinforcing those strips of vulnerable East Anglian coastline. Barbed wire fences, steel scaffolding erected on the beaches; like a vast stretch of scenic railway winding across the golden sands, railway lines embedded deep in concrete at the low-water line, and the entire area sown with land-mines, all contributed to a first line defence system. In July 1940 His Majesty King George VI visited Felixstowe, arriving by water from Harwich to inspect the defences and the 300-year-old Landguard Fort. One thing he must have been impressed with on his tour was the novel flame-gun. In an attempt to thwart Hitler's invasion of England – code-named 'Operation Sealion'; the overall purpose of this plan being, as Hitler recorded: 'To prevent England from being used as a base from which to continue the war against Germany' – a series of giant flame-throwers had been built into several strategically-placed cliff faces around the east coast, fuel being supplied to the weapon from a number of oil tanks also concealed along the cliff top. It was envisaged that if enemy invasion barges did manage to breach the Channel they would be met with a sea of blazing oil.

It wasn't only at sea that we find the introduction of flame-warfare, for the British authorities hit upon a novel idea of trying to destroy German industrial sites with the aid of fire balloons. Hugh Dalton, Minister of Economic Warfare, wrote in his memoirs[1]: 'I said it was common knowledge that the Germans had hidden many arms factories and other military installations in the Black Forest, and we were entitled to burn off the cover which concealed these legitimate targets.' The outcome was that much later in the war an attempt was made to set fire to the Black Forest, not by aircraft but by releasing small balloons, to be carried to their target area by the wind and there to turn into incendiaries as they fell. Unfortunately, the wind changed and these balloons were carried back to East Anglia, where several of them, on bursting into flames, did damage to young plantations of the British Forestry Commission.

Hitler issued his first orders for 'Operation Sealion' on 2 July 1940. Between that date and 17 September Britain awaited the invasion with bated breath. Her defences were gathered under the code-name 'Cromwell' and 7 September saw men standing ready and waiting for the next twelve days at their posts. During the first panic-stricken night a false alarm was sounded with bells being rung, bridges blown up and in East Anglia engineers planted batches of land mines along several important roads causing the death of a number of Guards officers.

[1]*The Fateful Years 1931-41*, Hugh Dalton, page 276.

Pill-boxes were also hastily constructed and not always to the best advantage – as local builders, with plans held the wrong way round, built them back-to-front, upside down and, at Brightlingsea, a couple were placed below the high-water mark causing them to be uninhabitable during high tides! More successful were the retractable machine-gun emplacements built at Martlesham Heath airfield. These tiny pill-boxes, entered through a manhole, were normally flush with the surface of the grass airfield and would prove no obstacle to a taxi-ing aircraft, but if an attack came they could be raised by hydraulic hand-pumps to provide stiff opposition to parachute troops or others who might make a landing[1].

As airfields were laid and while more permanent defences were being built, mobile air-raid shelters, allocated for the protection of men employed on defence works, were taken onto the wide open and shelterless fields. They were constructed from grocers' vans and builders' lorries converted into a Heath Robinson affair consisting of a wooden box-like superstructure, its cavity wall filled with loose pebbles, hopefully resistant to machine-gun fire at close quarters.

An example of the concrete pill-box which could be seen around the highways of East Anglia during the early 1940s.

[1] *East Anglian Daily Times.*

They were known as the Armadillo . . . named after a 'Central and South American burrowing animal possessed of a bony armour, indifferent vision and acute sense of smell and hearing.'

Building these defences meant transporting squads of labourers from all parts of East Anglia and a fleet of coaches was utilised to move the men from base to base. Petrol shortages were painfully acute during that time and Mr J.W. Sutton, of Sutton's Coaches, remembers, as a young lad, his father carting cans of petrol around the different sites in the back of his private car; the coaches consuming far too much petrol to be allowed to return to the home garage for refuelling. Later in the war these coaches carried German and Italian POWs to gather the harvest and fell timber.

During those early stages of the war much of Britain's defence force was heavily committed. East coast harbours and ports had to be defended somehow and in a lot of instances things were not as they first seemed! Around the Harwich/Brightlingsea/Walton-on-Naze area a number of submarines suddenly made an appearance. These had in fact been built at the Wivenhoe Ship Yard . . . made entirely of wood! Mr A.G. Bareham, a ships' carpenter who helped build these fifty-foot decoys, remembers that they did in fact represent the real thing, even down to a gun mounted on the bow. Built of match-boarding which was pinned to a skeleton framework, the 'submarine' resembled, at close quarters, an inverted rowing boat. It was so flimsy and fragile that when launched it whipped and warped so alarmingly that it was thought and feared to have broken its back. Once afloat they were then towed to their respective 'bases' to take up a defensive position. The one being shipped to the Walton backwaters unfortunately slipped its tow rope, being driven ashore into the scaffolding defences being erected along the Holland-on-Sea beaches. From a distance it must have truly looked like a genuine submarine, for a few nights later Lord Haw-Haw announced that 'The submarine pens now being built at Holland-on-Sea would receive a visit from the Luftwaffe.' Sure enough a machine-gun raid was carried out against the 'pens' within the week. Another time a decoy submarine lying off Harwich harbour was also attacked and the sentry mounted against the conning-tower – a straw-filled dummy garbed in a sailor-suit – was riddled with machine-gun bullets.

The presence of enemy agents lurking around the coastal areas of East Anglia could not be ruled out, for the authorities had in fact captured a couple whilst making a landing along the Suffolk coast in the early part of the war. However, not all were apprehended for one night a light two-seater German reconnaissance aircraft which crash-landed between Beccles and Bungay was discovered. Although evidence pointed to there being a passenger aboard the 'plane, the pilot swore that he had been alone. If there had been anyone he was never found. One agent was known to have spent his war around the Walton-on-Naze – Harwich area and he too was never apprehended. As a matter of fact British Military Intelligence knew the existence of most agents based in Britain and in a number of cases enrolled their services as double-agents, allowing them to send back to Germany snippets of both useful and useless information. Sometimes these XX-agents fed back information that the British *wanted* the enemy to learn about . . .

Apart from the XX-agent, East Anglia also played host to a special brand of under-cover agent. Acting as ARP, Observer Corps or, in one instance, as members of the Civil Defence, these men and women were responsible for tracking and logging wireless messages in and out of Britain. With their wireless equipment concealed in an innocent-looking suitcase – usually hidden beneath the bed – they monitored all recorded (and unrecorded) wireless traffic. These people, living in a twilight, make-believe world, were also employed in relaying messages to partisan groups working behind the enemy lines in Europe. On occasions they were also used in tracking down wireless stations of British-based enemy agents. Provided the spy stayed on the air long enough for them to get a cross-bearing on his set, they could plot his exact location within a very short while.

It wasn't all honey for these undercover agents for as they didn't work normal hours or ever seem to attend to their official duties, they came under a certain amount of suspicion and hostile scrutiny. Consequently when this happened the agent had to be shifted around from town to town or village to village. If they were unfortunate enough to be arrested and taken into custody a telephone call to a special number would soon result in their release and immediate removal from the district.

Before the war, during the balmy summers of 1938-39, private German aircraft and airliners of the Deutsche Lufthansa were suspected of taking reconnaissance photographs whenever they flew back and forth across the east coast. Captured German documents taken after D-Day confirmed these suspicions when secret Wehrmacht books and maps were found showing both aerial and ground photographs of almost every important town and city in the British Isles. Listed together with details of pumping and electricity

 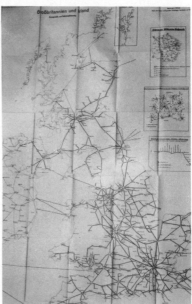

Left: Captured German maps and books showing photographs and important installations in Great Britain (the centre illustration gives details of an aerial view of Norwich).

Right: Another captured German map showing details of the telegraph network in Britain, c. 1940.

stations, hospitals, Town Halls, wireless masts and even early closing days, one found that an efficient Teutonic mind had even included the known population of each place listed. The maps gave details of telegraph and telephone lines and water pumping stations; one even gave the geological breakdown of our tiny island. The Germans had done their homework well! It wasn't only passengers aboard low-flying aircraft who spied out the land either, for another more dedicated group did sterling work as they hiked around the open countryside. These were youths of the *Deutsches Jungvolk* and *Hitler Jugend* who, while on hiking and camping holidays around the eastern and southern coast, professionally listed and noted places of interest both military and industrial. In some instances, when more detailed information was requested by the Abwehr, certain former BUF sympathizers assisted with the photographic details.

One of the war's best kept secrets must surely be the building and staffing of decoy sites built around East Anglia in an attempt to draw enemy bombing raids away from vital targets. So well kept a secret, in fact, that little or nothing was known about them until recently[1].

Known as 'Q', 'K' and 'Drim' sites, the original plan had been to build a series of top-secret decoy sites to cover important towns, ports, airfields and military installations.

The 'Q' sites – named after the British World War I famous decoy Q-ships – were usually built to resemble a dock or harbour, being equipped with flickering lamps, gantries, oil tanks and other paraphernalia of a dockyard scene. A 'K' site was equipped with dummy aircraft, bomb dumps, petrol dumps and a flare path, while the 'Drim' site was a flare path only, usually manned with only a minimum of service personnel.

Norwich was covered by a decoy site which, during a 'Baedeker' raid in 1942, received a load of incendiary bombs intended for the ancient city. The port of Ipswich was covered by a decoy site built in a field on the north side of the Ipswich to Felixstowe road, near the 'S'-bend between Nacton cross-roads and Levington Bridge. The officer in charge of this site had his HQ in the Martello Tower situated in the heart of Felixstowe. In here, with a battery of telex-printers and telephones, he would await the all-important signal which would tell him to light up the decoy site and order the smoke-troops based in Ipswich to start up their smoke-making machines to cover the town in a pall of heavy smoke. Although the Ipswich decoy site was never used in anger they did have a practice run. One over-zealous officer wanted to see if the smoke-troops, made up of conscientious objectors, could be relied upon to work the machines properly if and when the occasion ever arose. Setting up a practice exercise, the port of Ipswich soon vanished beneath a man-made cloud of smoke . . . only to have the wind change, sending sweeping clouds of choking smoke down into the town centre, causing the inhabitants to cough and splutter for the rest of the day.

When one stops and considers the 100-1 chance in deciding just *where* the enemy would strike and just *what* decoy site had to be lit up it all seems something of a hit and miss affair. As it transpired it wasn't such a gamble after all, for British intelligence had managed to procure a German cipher machine called Enigma as early as 1938. A Polish-Jew who had worked as a mathematician and engineer at the factory in Berlin where Enigma was produced had approached MI6 with an offer to sell his knowledge of the machine for £10,000[2].

With this knowledge the British built an exact replica of the German cipher machine which throughout the entire war was used to decode every important German battle order, flight plan and

[1]The author chanced to meet a former Intelligence Officer who had been in charge of the port of Ipswich decoy site . . . this gave him the vital lead to other sites around East Anglia.
[2]*Bodyguard of Lies*, Anthony Cave Brown.

proposed bombing raid. Churchill even knew in advance that Hitler was going to invade Russia . . . but never said a word. When Coventry was on the cards to be bombed, Enigma in Britain had laid the news on the Prime Minister's desk several days beforehand, but rather than risk letting the enemy know that he had broken their cipher he let the raid take place without warning the Coventry authorities. In that series of raids 554 citizens were killed and another 865 seriously wounded. A total of 50,749 houses were destroyed or damaged. The raids may well have been forecast in advance but there was little one could have done to stop them actually taking place, hence the introduction of the decoy sites.

Another 'Q' site was that built on the lower marshes near Shop Lane, East Mersea, in 1940-41. Planned by the Admiralty and erected with civilian labour, its main function was to cover the important mine-sweeper base at nearby Brightlingsea. It was controlled by a squad of six men based in a nearby pill-box cleverly concealed with earth and bracken to blend in with the surrounding countryside. The actual decoy buildings were constructed of wood and tubular steel covered with thin canvas and thatching allowing a glimmer of light to shine through when the unit was lit up at night.

One of the deep reinforced concrete bunkers which housed radar personnel at the Great Bromley site.

Rare pencil sketch of the East Mersea 'Q' decoy site built in 1939-40 to cover Brightlingsea minesweeper base. In the foreground are buildings of thatch and canvas which were equipped with flickering lamps and lanterns. Centre left are oil and water tanks linked with an explosive device. Drawn by one of the site guards, Mr Hubert Inman, in 1944.

Other lanterns were suspended on a rope near the water's edge to simulate marshalling yard lights on the move. Tanks of oil and water built on high gantries had been fitted with a remote-control mechanism allowing both oil and water to flow into a series of shallow ditches which surrounded the buildings when the need arose. To ignite the mixture, which in turn would catch light to the site, thus leading the enemy to believe he had successfully struck his intended target, a small bomb which was also remotely controlled had been placed beneath the tanks. Although never actually used in anger the base did once go up in a mass of flames. In summer, the grass around the site had the habit of growing very tall and wild and to perpetuate the illusion that the site was occupied the men used to cut the grass with sickles and scythes. Unfortunately, while doing so they cut through the mass of hidden wires which controlled the lights and explosives mechanism . . . rejoining the loose wires without the necessary blueprints didn't help matters for in the ensuing flash of short-circuited wires the entire base vanished in a cloud of smoke and flames. It had to be completely rebuilt.

Other sites existed around East Anglia; one on the Walton-on-Naze marsh built to cover the explosives factory on Bramble Island (two men were killed here when they tried to rescue a dog in a minefield), another at Great Bromley to cover Colchester railway station, and yet another at Bradfield. These 'Q' sites were under the command of Lt. Commander W.A.A. Greenwell, RNVR, based at Harwich.

Most of the sites were guarded by heavy artillery guns but so as not to arouse the enemy's suspicions the majority of them were camouflaged. The Ipswich site was guarded by a rail-mounted coastal defence gun hidden in a copse of fir trees. At least it *was* hidden until a series of practice fires completely denuded all the trees in the area. Another gun close by, however, remained hidden throughout the war, being enclosed in what looked like a farm store. The roof and upper half of the walls of this structure were mounted on rails and could be slid back to permit the gun to be elevated. Anyone interested can still see this building, but without the extended rails, standing between the A45 and the railway on the Ipswich side of the road leading to Stratton Hall and the Suffolk Yacht Harbour. It now serves as a farm store.

'K' and 'Drim' sites were, in the main, built to cover exposed airfields and the construction of bomb dumps, petrol installations, air raid shelters etc. was carried out by civilian workers. RAF personnel classed as Aircrafthand General Duties cleared the sites of scrub and undergrowth, then filled and levelled off the large craters. Dummy aircraft built of wood, tubular steel and canvas and constructed at the Shepperton film studios were delivered to the various sites around East Anglia and assembled by the airmen who then painted them with camouflage paint, applied the RAF roundels and set them out around the perimeter of the 'airfield'. As a former wartime RAF decoy site 'erk' Ray Howlett recalls: 'It was just like building an aircraft with a giant "Meccano" set . . . The wings etc. were the exact size of the actual aircraft and bolted together with bolts and wing-nuts.'

As it so happened, many of the men responsible for building and running the 'K' and 'Drim' sites hailed from Norfolk and Suffolk for, being natives, they seemed to know how to handle the 'nosey-parkers' who strayed onto the sites from time to time; for it took about three months to make a site fully operational. One such 'K' site was built on Cavenham Heath near the villages of Tuddenham and Cavenham, being a satellite for Mildenhall airbase. The 'aircraft' were Wellingtons or, as the RAF liked to call them, 'Wimpeys' – for at that period there were two squadrons of these aircraft based at Mildenhall still confined to carrying out leaflet raids over Germany. On the 'Drim' sites the men, on receiving the warning light, would touch off the flare path, then rush to take cover in a deep shelter built at the end of the 'runway'. Two such sites were built at Littleport near Ely, another being at Nacton near Ipswich, acting as a satellite for Martlesham Heath.

As war progressed and the allies started to build up a concentration of arms and troops in preparation for the forthcoming invasion, more decoy sites were built along the East Anglian coastline. In April 1944 a scheme under the code-name 'Fortitude South' involved the creation of a phantom invasion force, not merely of an army, but of an army group – an imaginary force of a million men and fifty divisions. In southern and southwestern England there were two army groups being assembled – Montgomery's 21st and Bradley's 12th. On D-Day the former would strike out for Normandy and the latter would follow up once the beachhead had been established. But to try and make the Germans believe that a third force – the First United States Army Group (FUSAG) – was assembling in south-eastern England with the intention of launching a major attack against the Pas de Calais, a series of dummy petrol dumps, pipelines, sewerage farms, hospitals, tank-parks and barracks were constructed around East Anglia.

To help foster this illusion a number of calculated leakages began to appear in the press and on the wireless.

'This is the American Forces Network. Here is *Sweethearts' Playtime*. Private M. of the 315th Reconnaissance Troop, 11th Infantry Division, on duty somewhere overseas, is twenty today, and here is the *Six Lessons from Madame Lazonga*, as requested by his fiancée, Miss R. of Great Neck, New York' . . . '2/Lt. N. of O. Falls Church, Va., on active service in England with the 9th Airborne Division, a sophomore of Jonn Hopkins, has announced his engagement to Miss P. of Norwich, England.'[1]

During the *Neptune* build-up for D-Day, German reconnaissance aircraft were 'allowed' to intrude over the FUSAG area. There, around harbours, river mouths and in tiny creeks ranging from Yarmouth to Lowestoft, the Norfolk Broads, the Orwell and River Debden, they spotted over 400 'landing craft' . . . from the air they looked the part, for with smoke coiling from their funnels, crews made up of over-age or unfit soldiers from units of the 4th Northamptonshires and 10th Worcestershires, and motorboats fussing back and forth disturbing the oil-slicked waters, they created an illusion of an invasion army gathering strength. In reality the craft were little more than canvas and wood mounted on a tubular scaffolding framework floating on oil drums. These too had been constructed at Shepperton film studios and brought to East Anglia by road.

Overhead, RAF units maintained constant fighter patrols as if to protect the armada below, allowing the odd enemy aircraft to filter through provided they were flying at above 33,000 ft, where it was impossible for their cameras to pick out any discrepancies or defects in the units.

Around Rendlesham Forest, south-east of Woodbridge, Suffolk, a vast conglomeration of rubber, wood, iron and cardboard buildings sprung up; on the River Debden a flotilla of 'invasion barges' lay moored, all strategically placed to perpetuate the illusion of a gathering army. The illusion did in fact work, for captured Luftwaffe records taken at the end of the war revealed that 'Q', 'K' and 'Drim' sites were still being listed as proposed targets.

A number of hush-hush projects were developed around East Anglia including experiments with rockets on the Walton-on-Naze marshes. Locals recall the time when the town was shaken to its foundations and the entire area lit up with a strange phosphorescent glow that turned the night into day as 'something' went off!

Top secret weapons were also developed in our part of the country,

[1]*Bodyguard of Lies*, Anthony Cave Brown.

Above: A cheque for One Pound Seven Shillings (£1·35p); just one of many paid out to returning servicemen after the war by a grateful town.

Below: Two examples of messages of thanks issued by King George VI and his daughter, Queen Elizabeth II. *Photo: Stan Shelley.*

for near Bedford a couple of 'boffins' perfected an underwater mine known as the 'Limpet', Colonel R.S. Macrae and Major C.V. ('Nobby') Clarke had perfected the mine but were having considerable trouble in producing a satisfactory fuse that would dissolve under water. As Colonel Macrae recalls: 'The next thing to do was to devise a delayed-action initiator which would cause this gadget to go bang in anything between half an hour and two hours after its

An example of a 'Victory' poster to be found hanging in the homes of 'Mr & Mrs Great Britain' in 1945. The flags are of the then Allies; list of campaigns are below. The open books bear a few lines of some of Winston Churchill's famous speeches.

installation. There was nothing on the market that would serve the purpose but it was simple enough to think up something . . . or so we thought! We went to all the big chemical people who made us a lot of pellets at great expense which didn't work. Then one day while working in Nobby's workshop I happened to pick up one of his young children's sweets that had been dropped on the bench. Popping it into my mouth, it didn't seem so bad – I'd never eaten an aniseed ball

before – and I was surprised just how long it took to dissolve. So I looked into this and found you could count on the time that each one took to dissolve. This was the thing we had been looking for. I rigged up a contrivance for drilling holes through the centre, which took a bit of doing, I must say, and then contacted Barratts the sweet people to order some more in bulk. While we were awaiting their arrival we combed Bedford, much to the children's disgust, buying up all the aniseed balls we could find.'

The next problem to temporarily stump the two scientists was to keep the fuse waterproof until the mine was needed. Once again a lot of head-scratching was needed before they hit upon the novel idea of using rubber contraceptives. Visiting all the chemist shops in Bedford and buying up all their stocks they met their requirements but at the same time earned themselves a dubious reputation!

During six years of war East Anglia had certainly witnessed a lot of strange things. Being in the front line, so to speak, the war had indeed been brought to her shores. Many strange stories have been told through these pages and a great many more have yet to be told . . . a number, like the mystery which surrounds Shingle Street, will have to wait some time to be told, but when they do eventually become printed, will help to complete the picture of East Anglia at War.

THE END

BIBLIOGRAPHY

English History, 1914-1945. A.J.P. Taylor.
The Defence of the United Kingdom. Basil Collier.
War Begins at Home (1940). Mass Observation.
Life & Times of Ernest Bevin. Alan Bullock.
The Day War Broke Out. Ronald Seth.
Invasion 1940. Peter Fleming.
The Last Ditch. David Lampe.
New Ways of War. Tom Winteringham.
The Protecting Power. Eugen Spier.
The First and the Last. Adolf Galland.
Ack Ack. General F. Pile.
Women in Green. Charles Graves.
Civil Industry and Trade. E.L. Hargreaves & Margaret Gowing.
Lord Haw Haw. J.A. Cole.
The Theatre at War. Basil Dean.
The Women's Land Army. V. Sackville-West.
If Their Mothers Only Knew. Shirley Joseph.
Science at War. J.G. Crowther & R. Whiddington.
Challenge of Conscience. Dennis Hayes.
The Battle of the V-Weapons 1944-45. Basil Collier.
Winston Churchill's Toyshop. Stuart Macrae.

ACKNOWLEDGEMENTS

First and foremost my heartfelt thanks to all those East Anglians who patiently answered lengthy questionnaires during six long years of research. Also those who supplied snippets of information which in turn led to a worthwhile story . . . without their help this book would not exist today. To the editors of *Essex Countryside Magazine, East Essex Gazette, Essex County Standard* and *East Anglian Daily Times*, my thanks for allowing me space in their letter pages. And although it is impossible to list everyone concerned I should especially like to mention the following: Bundesarchiv, Freiburg. Deutsche Dienststelle, Berlin. USA Information Service, London. Frau E. Sodtmann. Ministry of Defence. Douglas Salmon, Producer, BBC TV., Victor S. Wilson, S.P.R., A.I.L., Mr D.B. Nash, Imperial War Museum. Lt. Col. J.M. Langley, M.B.E., M.C., Lt. General Avi. Baron M. Donnet, C.V.O., D.F.C., Colonel R.S. Macrae, M.D.I., F.I. Mech. E., Group Captain Colin Gray, D.F.C., D.S.O., Captain Ian M. McLeod. Sir Peter Greenwell. Sgt. Flight Engineer Harold Curtis. Flt/Lt. Raymond Baxter. Mrs Rose Kennedy (USA). Robert Malster. Ray Howlett. Stan Shelley (Photographs). Mr Hubert Inman. Allan Jobson. Mr B. Smith. Malcolm (BAT) Batty. Mrs E.M. Atthill. Mrs Dorothy M. Gregory. Christopher R. Elliott. Mrs Margaret Windridge. Mr Leslie M. Petch. David Clarke, curator of Colchester Castle Museum. Staff of Clacton Public Library.